Evidence Found

An Approach to Crime Scene Investigation

Evidence Found

An Approach to Crime Scene Investigation

David M. Miranda

AMSTERDAM • BOSTON • HEIDELBERG
LONDON • NEW YORK • OXFORD
PARIS • SAN DIEGO • SAN FRANCISCO
SINGAPORE • SYDNEY • TOKYO
Academic Press is an imprint of Elsevier

Academic Press is an imprint of Elsevier
32 Jamestown Road, London NW1 7BY, UK
525 B Street, Suite 1800, San Diego, CA 92101-4495, USA
225 Wyman Street, Waltham, MA 02451, USA
The Boulevard, Langford Lane, Kidlington, Oxford OX5 1GB, UK

Notices

Knowledge and best practice in this field are constantly changing. As new
research and experience broaden our understanding, changes in research
methods, professional practices, or medical treatment may become necessary.

Practitioners and researchers must always rely on their own experience and
knowledge in evaluating and using any information, methods, compounds,
or experiments described herein. In using such information or methods they
should be mindful of their own safety and the safety of others, including parties for whom they have a professional responsibility.

To the fullest extent of the law, neither the Publisher nor the authors, con-
tributors, or editors, assume any liability for any injury and/or damage to
persons or property as a matter of products liability, negligence or otherwise,
or from any use or operation of any methods, products, instructions, or ideas
contained in the material herein.

ISBN: 978-0-12-802066-1

British Library Cataloguing in Publication Data
A catalogue record for this book is available from the British Library

Library of Congress Cataloging-in-Publication Data
A catalog record for this book is available from the Library of Congress

For information on all Academic Press publications
visit our website at http://store.elsevier.com

Typeset by TNQ Books and Journals
www.tnq.co.in

Printed and bound in the United States of America

Contents

Foreword

The field of forensics has never been black and white. The answer to many questions regarding the analysis of evidence can be summed up by the phrase "it depends on the case circumstances." Investigation at crime scenes in particular is an ever-evolving matrix of circumstances, and no two scenes will ever be treated exactly alike. Confounding the issue of the situational uncertainty is the fact that crime scene investigation can be conducted by multiple individuals and agencies. Like cogs in a wheel, each person has a different responsibility that fits together with the work everyone else is doing. From sworn First Responders to Forensic Specialists, Criminalists, and other nonsworn professional staff, everyone has their part to play.

For crime scene investigators (CSI), the collection, documentation, and preservation of evidence is the most crucial and significant aspect of their job. It is important for an investigator to think outside the box to successfully perform his or her duty, and that function does not stop at evidence collection; it extends to report writing and potentially testifying in court. A CSI generally only sees the aftermath of a crime, and it is the responsibility of that investigator to help put the pieces of what happened back together. Like putting together a jigsaw puzzle, these pieces will ultimately provide the jury with the big picture they need to make a decision in the case.

In keeping with the demands of the profession, the author of this publication has always been a man who could think outside the box and successfully convey his ideas to others. I first met David Miranda, the author, in a Forensic Science Academy that I attended after college. With his nearly 20 years experience in the field, he had no trouble morphing our group of 40 naive students into a reasonably functioning crime scene investigation team. Firm but not domineering, he instilled within us the importance of efficiency and teamwork. He had years of experience to call upon to impart relevant tips on how to be successful at locating the most probative evidence possible.

Many years have passed since I first met David, and I have followed his footsteps to become an instructor myself. Throughout the years of working with both First Responders and nonsworn professional staff, I consistently find that the most common questions I get involve requests for tips and tricks that I might have on how to better process items of evidence. This publication addresses that specific issue, which differentiates it from the large majority of textbooks available on the market today.

In his desire to reach a broader audience, Dave takes his vast experience working as a CSI in a city police agency, and as an overseas forensic consultant, to present the skills he has acquired. The aim of his text is not to give you a general overview of the job of a CSI, it is to help sharpen your skills as an investigator and present you a different way of approaching a crime scene. He congregates knowledge of specific techniques and successful methods of processing a wide variety of scenes that can only be gained by years of experience in the field.

This textbook covers a plethora of topics, but not in a traditionally covered manner. It expands upon topics not usually covered in crime scene investigation books, such as interagency cooperation and maximizing efficiency in a scene teeming with sworn and professional staff alike. The subject of how to locate and identify evidence is expanded upon with case examples and novel techniques. The dreaded topic of courtroom testimony is also covered, but instead of addressing the conventional basics of how to dress and act in court, the author goes further and tackles how to answer difficult questions and addresses the current challenges to the field of forensic science.

A crime scene tells a story of an interaction between suspect and victim, and it is the duty of forensic professionals to recreate that interaction based on the evidence that is found and collected. It is no small responsibility that the individual collecting and documenting evidence at the scene of a crime holds the potential to unlock justice for the victim and alter the fate of any potential suspect. This publication provides diagrams and case examples to exemplify ways to approach the scene in a logical and competent manner. For those of you who are interested in being more efficient and successful at crime scenes, this text is for you.

Allison Flattum, MS
Forensic Scientist

Preface

If you are a forensic practitioner who must respond to crime scenes, day in, day out, and all night long, then this work is for you. If you are someone with authority over the forensic portion of a criminal investigation or the forensic personnel involved, I believe you will find this volume helpful as an evaluative tool to anticipate issues before they negatively impact an investigation. And if you are someone who simply has long had a fascination with the world of forensics, either as a student or someone with a high interest, I believe you will find this informative and perhaps even a proverbial "peek behind the curtain" to the workings of a forensic investigation.

Forensics was not my original career choice but it was the one I spent the most time in 24 years. I was a founding member of my department's Forensic Unit when the switch was made from a rotational assignment for sworn personnel to a permanent career position for civilians. At that time, there were not that many career Forensic personnel and most of those were in larger agencies. But medium- and smaller sized police departments, nationwide, were realizing what many larger organizations had already proven: that forensics was becoming a field that was continually developing to the point that a department needed individuals who were solely dedicated to becoming experts in that field and who would be in position to be aware of and incorporate those developments as they happened. During my tenure, I was privileged to witness changes, additions, and developments as the field expanded in scope and impact, such as the introduction of DNA into criminal proceedings, the (now) common use of Ninhydrin over magnetic powder on paper (which does work, by the way, but not nearly as well as the chemical process) and, of course, the challenges currently faced in the field of fingerprint comparisons. I found myself involved in several high-profile investigations such as the 1993 Halloween Homicide in Pasadena, CA, the 2005 Glendale Train Wreck (assisting, by request, the Glendale PD Forensic Unit who were magnificent in the face of competing agencies agendas, but that is another story), a beheading, the usual assortment of mundane and profane scenes that any of us experience after enough years in the business and, of course, the endless hours in court whether sitting in the hall or actually testifying.

Mixed in between all of those events were the usual training classes, workshops, and conventions one attends to keep up with the advances in the field, learn new skills, and network. It was often at those events, in the company of fellow practitioners from other agencies, that I learned some of my best lessons as we traded on our experiences (and of course, the stories behind them). After 24 years with my department, I spent 21 months in Afghanistan in support of Operation Enduring Freedom as a contractor employing my forensic skills in a deployed environment. Due to that experience, I had the privilege of hearing of the experiences of practitioners from across our nation who were also there in support, as well as the privilege of supporting my country's war effort. My experience in such an environment proved, once and for all, that forensic practitioners are some of the best problem solvers in the world, needing to accomplish forensic tasks, often without all of the supplies traditionally on hand, within a timeline, and in an environment that was not, shall we say, user friendly. This leads us to this book. Over the years, many of our processes have not changed, such as the continued use of black powder on so many nonporous surfaces. Others have changed and continue to do so, such as the introduction of HFE as a carrier for Ninhydrin or the continued development of national standards for the various aspects of our profession. What also did not change over the years was the need to go the random event known as a crime scene and apply our developing protocols and procedures to a dynamic environment, which continue to change. Everyone has experienced the constant of problem solving while applying the latest knowledge to a crime scene event, large or small. And, occasionally, mistakes were made which we all hate. Any and every responsible member of the law enforcement community does, whether the mistakes are high profile or not. We work to prevent them, developing checklists and after-action reports. But one of the things I rarely saw was an examination into the thought process that goes on in an investigation, especially one that resulted in one or more errors. I am not writing of an examination into motivations with implications of corruption or even laziness but about the concept of "how do we know what we know?" as we apply our training, protocols, and experience in a given investigation. In philosophy, this is known as "epistemology," study of the theory of knowledge. A concept rarely associated with crime scene investigation but impacts it, all the same.

Like most social groups, those involved in the field of criminal investigation tend to develop patterns, practices, and habits that are employed repeatedly, mainly because they repeatedly work. And the vast majority of the time, experience confirms that these patterns and practices were appropriately developed and ought to be repeated in each investigation. But when something does not work I saw that, also like most social groups, our foundation of knowledge is the last place that is searched for issues.

There tends to be a focus on the negative results and the specific events that led to them. But there was rarely a look at the foundations of knowledge or experience to see if, perhaps, the negative issue began before the crime scene ever started. This is important because the difference between our social group and others is that ours is the one that can become the foundation that leads to the criminal prosecution of a person with lifelong ramifications. James Madison, our nation's fourth President, wrote in Federalist Paper #51 that "Justice is the end of government. It is the end of civil society. It ever has been and ever will be pursued until it be obtained, or until liberty be lost in the pursuit." What does that have to do with anything? In my own view, the field of forensics, in the field or in the lab, is as much a part of that drive for justice as are any decision of the Supreme Court or any other action of the criminal justice system. The only difference is scope. And even then, how many cases have been derailed because of a small detail resulting from an error? And in reviewing those errors, do we routinely examine the **reason** a decision was made, not just that the decision was in error? This belief in this philosophy formed the foundation of what became a career-long examination that resulted in this book.

In discussions with other practitioners I saw that there was a lot of "Yeah, we had a situation like that" that helped confirm this idea. After culling negative events or issues that seemed to be personality driven, I focused this book on event types or issues that seemed systemic and experienced by two or more agencies. I applied nonforensic training from an earlier career that focused, essentially, on evaluating and dealing with human systems, and applied that type of analysis to the event types and issues depicted in this book. So this is an epistemological approach, looking at how we know what we know or think we know and how that impacts positive and negative decision-making related to crime scene investigation.

Finally, you will note that the subtitle is "an approach to crime scene investigation." The main title is obvious: Evidence Found—the goal of every investigation is to find the evidence. But there is more than one approach to the concept and I know that mine is simply one among many. Hence, "**an** approach…" rather than "the best" or "the correct" or, etc. I hope that what I have written here will be helpful and inspire even deeper thought that will improve the process of crime scene investigations. The best criminalists in the world and the best lawyers in the justice system can do nothing if the evidence is not found. With that in mind, I have included several common problems with solutions that I have not seen elsewhere, developed through my own trial and error experience. One such problem area, for example, is working a scene with little or no light; many books advocate waiting until daylight, which is rarely an option for a medium- to small-sized department, which makes up most of law enforcement serving the nation, so what can be done? There are other similar problems I address, as well, including a list of Do's and Don'ts for First Responders that sprang from a request by our own officers years ago in an effort to prevent inadvertent scene contamination or evidence destruction. I also have added my own views and counsel on the "CSI Effect," Courtroom testimony, and the NAS Report, focusing on its current impact (at the time of this writing). Thank you for giving me your time to read this book and I hope you will find the time well spent, if for no other reason but to confirm that you have been doing the job right, all along.

Evidence Found
An Approach to Crime Scene Investigation
By David M. Miranda

Acknowledgments

As with many books, this one had its own generous portion of assistance along the way. There are many in the industry with whom I had discussed many of these ideas and concepts over the years and provided their own viewpoints and true stories, helping me to see that the issues on which this book is focused are universal. But a few agreed to go above and beyond the call of friendship and provided insightful critiques and suggestions, some even reading more than one draft. I thank the following people for that level of friendship and collegiality: Bethany Venable, Forensic Technician II, Riverside County Sheriff's Department, California; Carlton Fuller, Forensic Supervisor, Riverside Police Department, California; Allison Flattum, Forensic Scientist, Orange County Crime Lab, California; Cindy Edison Ritter, Forensic Specialist, Glendale Police Department Crime Lab, California; Vanessa Hohreiter, formerly of Tacoma Police Department Forensics, Washington and current owner/operator of Story Road Photography; and one or two others who prefer anonymity but to whom I am grateful, all the same. Each one of them helped me to stay on track with my original vision for the book and reflected back what they read, helping me to make my point and shedding the excess baggage. I also wish to thank Dr Susan Maros, Ph.D., whose feedback from a nonpractitioner point of view has demonstrated to me that the text and case studies were as engaging as I had hoped. Thanks to my son, Sean Miranda, who took my ideas seriously and created several demonstration graphics and the results were as if they were transferred directly from my own imagination onto the screen. Finally, I wish to thank my wife, Ann, who wanted me to resist any hyperbole born of gratitude for her support of this project so I will simply say thank you to her who is the love of my life for many years and many careers.

Introduction

The obvious cannot be overstated.

This is the reason we have an unending supply of textbooks and resource works in this field. And each of us, having had very similar training regardless of geographic location or whether our level of service has been Local, County, State, or Federal, has learned unique lessons. Our goals are the same; find the evidence and process it correctly. Our problems are also very similar; how to perform the work that we do with the limited resources at hand and still deliver a quality result. As of this writing, the economic environment has negatively impacted the forensic field in terms of shrinking budgets, rosters, everything but the workload. The usual and not unrealistic approach is to "work smarter." If we are going to do that then I believe it is healthy to reexamine what that looks like. To that end, I add my own contribution.

There are many books and instructional videos that cover basic and advanced techniques in Forensics as it applies to crime scene work and latent print lab work. This book is not so much about how to do a forensic investigation or process a crime scene from a mechanics or techniques approach, but is about one way of establishing how to think about such an investigation. In effect, this is my attempt to establish a productive epistemology of crime scene processing. Just as officers work long and hard to acquire and establish a tactical mind-set, we must work equally hard to establish a *Forensic Mind-set*. Many believe that if we learn all of the right processes and practical skills that we have it, and largely we do. However, many times, evidence items can be missed and evidence processes can be misapplied. The reasons may not be as obvious as one may surmise. A review often establishes what went wrong and who is responsible but not, necessarily, the REASON it happened. It can be very difficult to review thought patterns when the usual point of any investigation is the establishment of blame. It is the aim of this work to go beyond that type of process and provide a framework for an approach to investigations in which we are consciously aware of our own thought and decision-making processes and, subsequently, adopt a better set of benchmarks for after action review that are intentionally problem-solving in nature.

In working to establish what I am calling a "Forensic Mind-set," it needs to be noted that there are other ways then what I will be describing in the following pages and I will readily concede that point, if someone wants to make it. It is my belief that in many areas of our profession there is more than one right answer and this one happens to be mine; borne of my particular set of experiences, training cycles, discussions, and self-evaluations. It is not enough to want to do a good job or even to know HOW to do a good job. One must be able to get to that mental state where one does a good job by nature and, more importantly, knows the reason that they have done so. We may take the time to plan for a process but we do not always take the time to establish the practical and philosophical foundation for those processes. We will, more often than not, get things right but not always for the right reason. It will be my contention that when we take the time to establish such a foundation, we are much less likely to make those embarrassing and, at times, tragic errors, which we are all trying to avoid. While I will readily admit that this may sound a bit esoteric, i.e., philosophies and epistemologies of crime scene processing, I ask the reader to bear with me and, if necessary, indulge me a bit. If I am right, this could go a long way to improving the work product that results from the collaborative effort that always goes into a police investigation, even the smallest ones.

If, while digesting the concepts and examples in this book, the reader's reaction is to mentally respond with "it's ALL Critical, it's ALL important, just do EVERYTHING" or some other version of similar response, I would submit that any law enforcement professional's honest self-assessment should dissuade one from what is, essentially, an emotional rather than a passionate response. By all means, I would agree with the appropriate place of passion in our work, but we cannot let investigative decisions be run by them any more than we can let fear drive the vehicle. We make decisions on the nature, importance or value, or other matters related to evidence and we do it all the time. What this book does is look at what some professions refer to as "sacred cows," values, practices, ideas, procedures that while time-honored and even time-tested may not always be the best or most productive approach for every situation. We do them because that is what we know.

Allow me to encourage the reader to examine their own paradigm of investigative philosophy. We all have one; we just do not necessarily call it that. For all of us, it is not enough to say "my method works for me" without knowing the reason: Is it because we are comfortable? Or is it because if I use your method that it will work for me as well as it does for you? What I ask, as you give of your time to read this text, is for you to allow me to challenge your paradigm with one purpose in mind…improving our collective ability of the solving of a crime to bring the appropriate party to the justice system. If, after such challenge and examination, the reader is able to articulate rational and logical reasons that their respective methodologies work for them and decide any approach I offer is not productive, I would be content because then it is a conscious choice after careful consideration. We must always examine our paradigms if we are going to be involved in the fluid world of criminal investigations.

The obvious cannot be overstated.

List of Figures

Chapter 1

The Evidence Search—Where It All Begins

Chapter Outline

ABSTRACT

Review of four basic methods of evidence searching forming the foundation of crime scene investigations. Introduction of the concept of an "intentional planning phase" to begin a scene investigation, intention being a conscious choice not an automatic thought process, characterized by a "direct affirmative statement"; i.e., "this is what we are going to do and the reason we are going to do it." A Case Study of how issues in evidence search could have been mitigated by an intentional planning phase. Develop a systemic approach. Fifteen minutes of intentional planning saves more time than simply working faster or harder.

KEYWORDS: Evidence search patterns; Forensic mind-set; Intentional planning.

A philosophy of crime scene investigation

It may be tempting to skip to the next chapter where I offer some practical evidence search techniques, but I ask the reader to stay with me. A review of some things we already know will be productive and that review will form the foundation of what I have previously referred to as a Forensic Mindset.

Any investigation begins with a search for evidence, once all other emergent items have been taken care of and secured to the limit of practical ability. Much of the time, the evidence is readily apparent. A gun, a pool of blood, expended cartridges, a vehicle, and the list could fill the rest of a book so I won't belabor that point. There are many protocols and practices for evidence search methodologies and they seem to fall into basic categories. For purposes of this work I will use the terms Lane, Grid, Circular, and Free Association. I will define what I mean by the use of these terms and if you associate a different term for each description, please do so as you read. I also accept the fact that some of the following methodologies may have subsections within the terms and it is not my intention to delve into them with this book.

A **Lane** search will be defined as one in which the scene is divided into (ideally) straight avenues of approach, beginning at the outermost area of the scene. The avenues may or may not be physically marked out and they will tend to have a defined width that is within the reasonable ability of the search participant to fully view any possible item of evidence within it. It has been described as the "bowling alley" or the "laned highway" approach, using a width of generally 10 feet, but it can be smaller or larger depending on the terrain and other limitations.

A **Grid** search will be defined as one in which the scene is divided into squares of varying widths, thus marking it out like a chess or checkerboard. This can be done visually, such as with string, or simply with verbal guidance for on-scene personnel. Depending on the human resources and equipment available, each person may be assigned a section of the grid; the scene may be searched by an agreed upon sequence of grids, or some combination of those approaches. Grid searches can also be vertical, such as those that can occur during the investigation of a clandestine gravesite.

A **Circular** search will be defined as one in which the investigator circumnavigates the crime scene in a manner that defines a series of concentric circles. Most circular searches will begin at the outer perimeter and work inward toward the approximate center of the scene; however, many have made cogent arguments for searches to begin at the perceived center of the scene (the dead body, for example) and work outward.

A **Free Association** search has also been called a "path of evidence" search. This will be defined as when obvious evidence, such as a firearm left by a perpetrator, is used as a starting point. A visual examination from that vantage point will then lead to other associated items, with the path being established by where the next discovered evidence is located. It is, more often than not, the methodology that is usually employed, largely because the evidence has presented itself at a scene in a manner that is easy to find using that method. It is also the most natural manner of locating items and is often the one most consistent with the perpetrator's path of travel and the items can be very obvious in many scenes.

As any experienced forensic investigator can attest, each method has its own advantages and drawbacks. It is clear that we all share the same caution about not letting the obvious evidence distract us from the other, less obvious, evidence items, whatever those may be. Despite this caution and our best efforts, many times that is exactly what happens. The size of the scene, visual obstacles, human resource issues, equipment issues, and even sociopolitical issues can all have an impact in the application of the various search techniques to a given scene.

So what is the solution? Well, the wrong answer would be to simply, "try harder" or "work harder" or "(fill-in-the-blank) harder." Unfortunately, this is the usual solution to a review of our mistakes. We may successfully identify the specific protocol, practice, or policy that was violated that led to the error and then simply resolve to "try harder." Even with the best of intentions, I contend that this practice may have practical value for a disciplinary approach, but it may not be the best problem-solving one. These problems can be anticipated and overcome during the planning phase of a forensic investigation. Some may be saying, "Planning phase? What planning phase?" The potential success of any venture, including crime scene investigation, is increased with planning.

FIFTEEN MINUTES OF PLANNING CAN SAVE HOURS OF PROBLEMS

Crime scene work needs an actual and defined planning phase that provides a framework for conducting the investigation. Certainly, subsequent events and evidence discoveries can compel the reevaluation of any plan and this is appropriate. Many times, however, planning consists of a quick overview of the scene followed by an immediate attack of the scene with a reliance on training, experience, and good teamwork for any necessary adjustments. From that point, decisions are made "on the fly" and for the majority of our cases this practice works because of the ability, training, and professionalism of those involved. This would apply to most, if not all of us. However, I am suggesting that this approach is a potential doorway to problems that, fortunately, rarely occur. But sometimes, the doorway is taken and when it is we can miss the reason that the mistake occurred.

The "plan as you go" approach (for lack of a better term) is an existential approach in which the problems of the immediate moment receive our attention. We, subsequently, adjust as we go, thus believing that we are looking ahead because we are adjusting for whatever problem presents itself during the investigation. This approach works a vast majority of the time, which is the reason we do it. It is my contention that the inclusion of an intentional and specific planning period in which we are not processing for prints, packaging evidence, or even doing an additional evidence sweep, lays a firm, reviewable, and cogent framework for an investigation. Such a practice can yield a crime scene mindset that is focused both on the immediate (existential) needs of the scene and on the scene as a whole work product. During this planning period, multiple viewpoints are welcomed and discussed as problem areas can be foreseen and specifically accounted for. Processing issues are voiced and the crime scene team can free itself from what can be called the "tyranny of the urgent." By all means, anything truly urgent (such as a wet shoeprint on a hot pavement) should be dealt with immediately. However, a planning approach can give a perspective on things that, at first, seem very urgent but can end up being lowered in priority after a short rational discussion of the matter. It can even be decided ahead of time whether to perform a given process or procedure twice, intentionally.

INTENTION IS A CONSCIOUS CHOICE NOT A DEFAULT SETTING

During the planning phase, intentionality must be a conscious choice and it should never be assumed that it is present. Many times we do things out of excellent habits and well-established and correct procedures, but in the previous case study, all concerned personnel argued that both of these things were followed and, therefore, someone missed their job and missed the evidence. This may have been true, within a limited scope, but this knowledge is not problem solving. The scene responders and subsequent personnel saw the shell casing, the blood, and the bullet entry point and wanted to immediately "get to work" so the scene (parking lot) could be freed for the apartment complex residents. All of this was done with the best of intentions and while some may argue that the residents will simply have to understand the circumstances, our collective circumstance includes the reality that social and political concerns can and do impact a given investigation. That is all the more reason to be more *consciously intentional* in a crime scene investigation. Before I offer the following as a case in point, I need to note that the agencies involved, dates, locations, names, and any other identifying information have been redacted to maintain focus on the issue/example at hand and for the victim's privacy. This will be true for all case studies presented throughout this book.

CASE STUDY 1: CARTRIDGES? WHAT CARTRIDGES?

The scene was a shooting investigation on a city street in which, at the time, the victim was injured. At that time, there were a series of drive-by shootings stretched over a period of several weeks that appeared to be gang-related, but the individual events were not necessarily related to each other. The victim had been found in the street after witnesses reported hearing shots fired. Some reported hearing a vehicle but not everyone did. After the victim had been removed by paramedics and by the time that forensic personnel had been called to the scene, the crime scene tape had been placed, contained to the general area of the victim with the street being blocked off for the investigation. The victim's bloody clothing, with bullet holes in various places, remained on the street and a nearby vehicle appeared to have a bullet strike that would be more closely examined during the investigation (Figure 1.1). Figure 1.1 depicts the details of this case study. The search began for additional bullet strikes on nearby houses to ascertain direction of possible travel of a possible vehicle as well as witnesses who were more specific. During the investigation, forensic personnel were aware that one witness was certain that the sound of the shots came from south of the location of the current scene. They were told by the personnel on the scene that the witness had, in fact, been interviewed and was not considered credible due to the fact that it was the only statement to that effect and that there were other, unspecified, reasons to question the credibility.

Forensic personnel applied a bullet trajectory angle rod to the bullet strike on the vehicle and the angle pointed to the south of the current scene. At this point, the forensic personnel, despite objections by some, traveled the path of the trajectory and located several spent cartridges in the street approximately 75 feet from the initial scene. There was, of course, a level of professional embarrassment among personnel over this discovery. The scene was appropriately expanded and a new evidence search was begun, guided by a

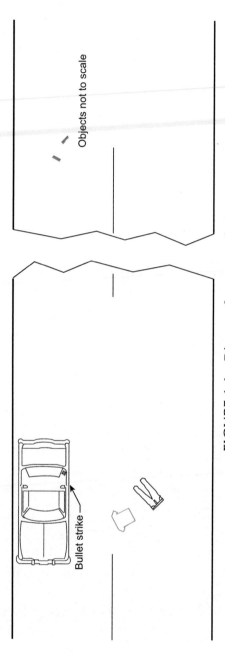

FIGURE 1.1 Diagram for case study 1.

more complete understanding of the sequence of events as now shown by the totality of the evidence.

Case Study 1 Analysis

The evidence search method used in the previous case study was Free Association aided by the use of forensic equipment (trajectory rods) to, literally, point investigators in the right direction. When such cases are reviewed, a problem-solving approach is very important. A blame approach is not helpful—satisfying at times, but not helpful. Fortunately, no one saw the need for disciplinary action, just a revisit of thought processes to ascertain the reason(s) that the single witness was not considered credible and no evidence search was conducted south of the location. It was determined that the decision to discount the witness was based on the fact that no other witnesses reported anything similar. A circular thought process can form the foundation of a presumptive theory in an investigation. The presumption that a witness will not be considered credible because of the presumptive theory and the witness account offered does not support that theory is, therefore, not credible. This is an example of how epistemology impacts a crime scene investigation in a negative way. Not "why" but "how" did we come to an unproductive conclusion?

Many may take the position of "how hard would it have been to send someone to check out the single witness statement to verify it?" However, this is simply another metaphorical doorway that can lead to a blame approach as well as an application of Free Association without considering whether it is the most productive use of available resources. The actual review used a cognitive approach that examined the individual and group thought process that occurred in which evidence was almost missed. If anything was missed it was planning, focus, and intentionality. There was an immediate search for evidence without ascertaining what the current theory may have been so the search plan, while understandable, was assumed without it being directly stated. Such an articulated statement of plan or intent is something I will call a direct affirmative statement; i.e., *this is what we are going to do and here is the reason we are going to do it.* A direct affirmative statement would most likely have caused personnel to question the initial premise. It was also temporarily forgotten or neglected what the bullet hole could reveal in the investigation due to a focus on apparent immediate aspects of the investigation. The bullet hole was half of the answer. In this case, a focus on the bullet hole inadvertently caused a pause in the evidence search without investigating the other half of the answer a bullet hole can provide. The remaining half of the answer is, of course, determined by the trajectory rods which, if used earlier in the investigation, would have saved personnel a certain amount of unnecessary effort, i.e., a canvass search of the entire street for casings. There were excellent intentions and, fortunately, a positive result, but a need for more intentionality.

So, if a planning meeting had occurred what issues could have been raised? What might it have looked like? Someone may suggest that the perimeter was too small. Perhaps it would be queried as to whether an exit hole from the bullet had been located or even looked for. Might a contingency plan have been developed in the event that the expected shell casing was NOT located in the immediate area? Do we plan for what to do in the event we do NOT find evidence that logic suggests should exist in a certain space? Without a plan we will apply whatever solutions come to mind regardless of their productivity to the case. This increases stress and decreases work product. A planning meeting can serve as a window into our thought processes by which we can anticipate these concerns in a relatively short time and account for them before they negatively impact an investigation. In the case study, it may be deduced that the right decisions were being made at the wrong time and with the best of intentions. A planning meeting can place those right decisions in a productive order. Further, whether your agency runs by a checklist, one person in charge, or any other methodology, voicing plans using direct affirmative statements and not being afraid to state or question the obvious allow us to examine the planned practices and procedures free of the natural myopia that can occur once each member attends to his/her respective tasks. Most importantly, such an intentional approach can help to ensure a sequential approach to a scene after all factors have been openly discussed. Some may object that such a meeting is unnecessary among crime scene professionals. I would offer that if one is holding such a thought then, no matter the skills, one is inviting disaster. Is it possible to go through an entire career without this approach and avoid any and all missteps? I would concede the point in the affirmative. But I would also ask what reason there is not to conduct a brief crime scene meeting that is planned and intentional? It is adaptable to any and all scenes, can serve to avoid duplication of effort UNLESS duplication is planned and intended, and lessens the overall time because evidence areas can be prioritized (a subject area to be covered in a subsequent chapter).

Professional illusionists have enjoyed long careers counting on the fact that, psychologically, people tend to see and hear what they expect to see and hear. We police professionals are no different except that we, at times, put the illusion on ourselves. Although incompetence, lack of training, lack of resources, or even extreme fatigue can be pointed to in many instances, it is a mistake to always look to those explanations and think the problem has been solved. A systemic approach that does not rely on intentional planning but allows success or failure to rest solely in the hands of the human resources involved fails those human resources. A systemic approach that resists impatience and outside pressure and intentionally plans its way through an investigation allows time for those same human resources to recognize potential failure before it even occurs. **Fifteen minutes of intentional planning can save hours of problems**.

Chapter 2

Evidence Search Techniques—Tips and Tricks

ABSTRACT

Maximizing our natural limitations. Nine recurring problematic situations in crime scene evidence search with tips and tricks to mitigate those situations: (1) Determining where evidence is and is not; (2) Field testing of theories; (3) Dealing with shell casings in grass at night; (4) Suspects wearing gloves; (5) DNA from areas already processed for latents; (6) Using magnetic powder on metal surfaces; (7) Review of old technique for night searching; (8) Introduction of new method for night search aka the Miranda technique; (9) Indoor search when there are no lights.

KEYWORDS: Dense shrubbery; Magnetic powder; Night searches; Tips and tricks.

Maximizing our natural limitations

Intentionality, planning, and direct affirmative statements are sound concepts that can support the techniques applied to a criminal investigation, maximizing the human resources available to that task. I believe the reader will agree that the best planning still needs the best means to accomplish any stated goals. There is no evidence unless we find it and while the basic approaches, as noted in the previous chapter, form the foundation for all evidence searches, there are special situations that have been shown to negatively impact our efforts. I will delineate a few of these situations that I have found recurring over numerous investigations and offer simple solutions to those situations.

SITUATION 1—KNOWING WHERE EVIDENCE IS NOT

When we are searching for evidence it can be helpful to be aware of areas where we know evidence will NOT be found. Some things are obvious, such as the bottom of a swimming pool (that has just been cleaned) for latent prints. Looking there for prints is, of course, a ridiculous idea, but it does prove the point that there are, in fact, areas of a scene that *can*, in good conscience and best practices, be ignored. Any judge or jury would not question that decision, but there are other, less obvious, situations than can be problematic in our approach. The application of logic and deduction is an invaluable tool in those situations. Awareness of this concept can help the crime scene investigator focus efforts in productive areas and avoid the unnecessary expenditure of time and energy.

As an example, let us examine a very common evidence search situation: that of determining and addressing the path of access and egress of a suspect to a given scene. When the path of a suspect is in the process of being determined, with the obvious goal of seeing if the individual left anything of evidentiary value during their traverse of an area, evaluating the area itself is a value that is often overlooked.

Examine the following two photographs.

In the first photograph (Figure 2.1) the concrete is free of debris and the dense shrubbery has a normal appearance. In the second photograph (Figure 2.2) one can see debris on the ground in front of the shrubbery and there is a slight visual difference in the shadows from the sunlight. The photographs were taken at mid-day and were one minute apart. Figures 2.3 and 2.4 show the debris field in greater detail, as well as a view of the physical state of the shrubbery in the second photograph.

It is clear that there was a disturbance in the shrubbery caused by the passage of a physical object against

FIGURE 2.1   Dense shrubbery, undisturbed.

FIGURE 2.2 Dense shrubbery after physical disturbance.

FIGURE 2.3 Detailed side view of Figure 2.2.

FIGURE 2.4 Indentation in shrubbery, physical disturbance.

it or over it. If we found this at a scene then our efforts could reliably focus on this area for possible evidence caused or left by the perpetrator. Absent these clear indicators, we can see that any detailed examination of this area is highly unlikely to yield any significant results. If this is in the area of the crime scene do we ignore it? Not necessarily, but based on this analysis (which takes much less time to process mentally than it does to write it or read about it) we could reliably place this area near the bottom of our list of "things to do" at a crime scene. There is no indication that the dense shrubbery is an area of suspect activity and, therefore, does not merit our primary efforts. Many times, the lack of this analysis causes the crime scene investigator to pursue all areas equally, causing an unnecessary expenditure of time and resources when a moment of analysis can focus the efforts of those involved, yielding results that are of greater value to the investigation.

SITUATION 2—FIELD TESTING OF THEORIES

I had a crime scene conundrum. It was a late night scene at the rear of a bank. There was, naturally, an ATM attached to the building with a ramp leading away from it toward the parking lot. At the bottom of that ramp a shooting resulting in death had occurred. The victim had as many wounds as there were expended casings on the ground and there were no exit wounds. The real question area was that, while the casings were all of the same caliber, four were in a group within 18 in of each other and one was over 6 ft away. All of the entry wounds to the victim were in the front. This led to numerous attempts to reconstruct the sequence of events, especially since witnesses who had heard the shots all insisted that all shots were fired in rapid succession. How does one explain the "stray" casing that is so far away from the others? Did we have two shooters, which was the favored theory at the time? Were the witnesses wrong as to the sequence of shots? Of course, that would mean that they were ALL wrong, a concept that is not impossible but requires a certain "leap of faith" for any investigator. Movement by the shooter was possible but this called for a rapid movement from one spot to another to cover over 6 ft and, depending on how one read the evidence, either the shooter shot several times, moved, and then shot once more or the other way around, all with great rapidity. Two shooters worked and we would have to wait until arrests to determine why one shot only once and the other shot multiple times but the placements were at odds with the apparent entry angles of the victims wounds. A conundrum that, possibly, would have to wait until a coroner's report and a hoped for ATM video before a resolution could hope to be entertained. However, my partner and I noticed that the surface on which the shell casings were resting was different than the parking lot surface.

The first photo (Figure 2.5) is concrete with small smooth stones inserted for texture and consistent with the original surface of the scene referenced here. The second photo (Figure 2.6) is typical of asphalt in roads and parking lots. The expended casings were all on the area that had concrete similar to that depicted in the first photograph. We reasoned that an empty shell casing, absent its load of gunpowder and projectile, would bounce and that there may be a correlation that

FIGURE 2.5   Pebbled concrete surface.

FIGURE 2.6   Typical asphalt surface.

explains the shell casing placement at rest. We decided
to conduct a brief on-scene experiment. Using a retract-
able ballpoint pen, we depressed the top to "load"
the spring and dropped it from a height of approximately 4 ft so that it would land on its top and cause
it to depress and actuate the spring, approximating the
spring that might occur from an empty shell casing
with the energy from an ejection from a firearm. We
were not looking for an exact replication of ejection
results but, instead, were seeking what could be called
a proof of concept.

We conducted this experiment on the asphalt and
found that the pen would come to rest within a radius of
12 to 14 in from the point of impact. This is illustrated
in Figure 2.7. The pen would also behave very predictably in that it would bounce once, with no turnovers of
any sort, and the only random action was the direction.
After conducting this same experiment on the concrete surface (away from the immediate scene but the

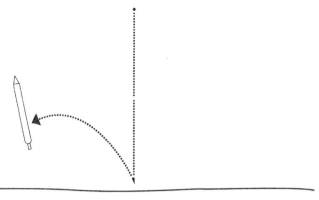

FIGURE 2.7   Typical trajectory of pen impact and bounce on asphalt surface. *Sean Miranda.*

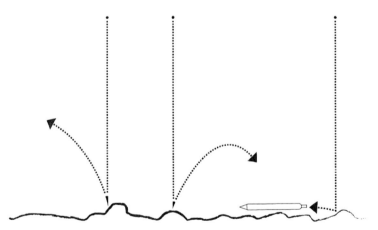

FIGURE 2.8   Various trajectories of pen impact on pebbled concrete surface. *Sean Miranda.*

same pebbled concrete) we found that the results were inconsistent and unpredictable. This is illustrated in Figure 2.8. At times the pen would simply come to an immediate rest with no bounce. At other times it would bounce at odd and unpredictable angles away from the point of impact. At one point, it bounced well over 6 ft away from the impact point. For us, this constituted the proof of concept. Was it possible that this ejection pattern could have happened without movement by the shooter? Yes, well within the realm of possibility. This experiment also let us know that the witnesses, who insisted that there was no pause in sequence of shots, were reliable in their recollection as this now demonstrated that such an action was possible despite the anomaly of the single expended shell casing. Further investigation was needed, of course, but the subsequent ATM video showed that there was, in fact, a single perpetrator involved. What conducting such an on-scene experiment could accomplish was that it prevented investigators from unnecessarily disregarding witness recollection and from focusing on a single theory of two shooters when one was, in fact, quite possible. On-scene experimentation is not possible or practical in most instances, but, the crime scene investigator who is always evaluating and thinking can recognize a situation when it presents itself and the value that such an experiment can have to an investigation.

SITUATION 3—GRASS, SHELL CASINGS, AND NIGHT

One of the most challenging situations is when those three things come together. I should note that I am referring to grass at lawn height. Most of the time, a daylight scene does not present the unique issues that a nighttime scene does, especially when searching for shell casings on a lawn. The problem is compounded by the fact that grass is also reflective. Not as much as your average shell casing but enough that, without proper technique, a shell casing can be overlooked, missed, or stepped on (making the daylight search even harder). To meet this challenge, I developed the practice of what I called "Tuning Your Eye." Most of the time, we know what something looks like and we find it because it matches our memory. The same thing occurs with the search for expended shell casings and, on a common surface such as asphalt or concrete, there is little variation between one location and the next so that our mental reference point serves us well. However, a grass lawn is not as common as one might think. Take a moment to look at a square foot area of your own lawn and two of your neighbors' lawns and you will see that, from afar, they are all green. Up close, they can be quite different in texture, depth, and density, even if the grass is the same type. Remembering this can save the investigator a great deal of frustration. I recommend carrying a brass shell casing, an aluminum one, a rifle caliber shell casing, and wadding of a shotgun. Place your initials on these items to distinguish them from anything else. When faced with a grass lawn, pick an area next to the chosen entry point of the lawn and be as certain as possible that there is no evidence at that location. Next, turn your back to the lawn and have someone toss the shell casing in that area. They can mentally mark where it is in the event that your tuning fails on the first attempt (a possibility). Turn around and commence your search for your test casing. What you are doing is acquainting your optical process with what an expended shell casing will look like on *this* lawn. Once you find it, your natural mental processes will automatically store this information as a reference point and when you conduct the rest of your search, the optical process will use the stored reference point and this lawn will now be as familiar to your mental process as an expended shell casing. Musicians will often speak of having to tune their instruments depending on the venue, even when they go from backstage to front, and this is an extension of that same concept. You are tuning your instrument, the eye, to the venue, the grass.

SITUATION 4—SUSPECTS WEARING GLOVES (LATENT PRINTS)

This situation is most common in property crimes. During the processing of the scene for prints, we see nothing or smears or a glove pattern. We know that none of this will be useful in identifying a particular perpetrator. The question is: Do the gloves ever come off? The answer is, yes, at times they do. Although it may seem like an odd use of the term, the application of ergonomics can be of help here. In a property crime, think of the structure and the areas of activity within that structure that is burgled as the working environment. The equipment used by the perpetrator will be their favored tool(s) of entry and, when chosen, gloves. The specific type will be dependent on the personal preference of the individual. Examining this criminal activity in this manner there is one thing (among many) that we can deduce: At some point during this activity and in a normal temperature environment provided by the structure, the gloves will cause a rise in body temperature in the hands. Perspiration can cause the gloves to become difficult to manipulate. Depending on the individual, that situation can cause enough discomfort so that the gloves will be removed in order to return to a comfortable state in which to work. If they choose not to, the activity itself becomes more difficult. As a test of this concept, I invite the reader to read this text and partake of their favorite beverage for 5 min while wearing the gloves of their choice. Detail work such as turning a page or rifling through a jewelry box becomes challenging, at the very least.

In those times when the gloves do, indeed, come off, is there a way to determine when or where in the scene that has occurred. Or do we simply dust everything until we come up with prints? That option may become necessary in the course of the investigation; however, here is what we can do to maximize our effort and minimize issues for the victim. By examining the activity of the perpetrator we can determine what I have come to call the "point of deepest penetration" where I define "penetration" not by distance from the point-of-entry but by the amount of activity that was performed. It is most often at that point that the level of discomfort compels the individual to remove the gloves, thereby leaving prints to be found. For example, a room in which a single jewelry box was opened displays minimal activity. A desk in which every drawer was opened and the contents ransacked displays maximum activity. If the jewelry box is on the other side of the building from the point-of-entry and the desk is in the room next to the point-of-entry, I would submit that, in terms of activity level and its impact on the individual involved, the desk is the point of deepest penetration of the location and the point where one is most likely to locate prints. Therefore, if one does not find useful prints at the point-of-entry, the desk (in this example) would be the next place to look. It has been my experience that when I've applied this concept, I can then proceed forward and backward from that point. At times, I have been able to find the very area where the gloves were removed. Generally, if you do not find prints at that deep point of activity, then it is highly likely that you have an individual who withstood the discomfort and left their gloves on through the duration of their activity.

SITUATION 5—SUSPECTS WEARING GLOVES (DNA)

In reference to the previous section, Situation 4—Suspects Wearing Gloves (Latent Prints), smudge or glove marks may have been found on the items or areas that have been dusted for prints. If so, then DNA is possible. (My thanks to Allison Flattum, Forensic Scientist for the Orange County Sheriff's Crime Lab in California, for this updated information based on studies she has performed.) The individual wearing the gloves will still be contacting areas that transfer cellular material, such as the face or hair, to the gloves and, subsequently, to the items handled that are being processed for prints. Further, it was many years ago that DNA testing techniques were refined to the point that DNA could still be recovered even after an item was processed with conventional fingerprint powders. This means that while it may be determined that the gloves never came off, the smudges that have been recovered are viable sources for DNA testing. A simple swab according to your department's collecting protocols will be sufficient to work with for the criminalist.

SITUATION 6—MAGNETIC POWDER USAGE: METAL

This section presumes either that you are compelled to process a surface at the scene or that you have already applied cyanoacrylate to the surface in a lab setting. The reader is likely familiar with the normal uses of magnetic powder. It is still largely taught that magnetic powder should never be used on metal. However, the proper application of magnetic powder on a metallic surface, particularly if it is painted, can yield results that are of significantly greater contrast than if regular or bichromatic powder was used. I was taught a technique over 20 years ago by a deputy from the Los Angeles County Sheriff's Department (whose name I no longer remember, apologies) that I have found invaluable. First, after loading your magnetic wand with magnetic powder, brush it lightly over the surface, making certain to have no physical contact of the wand itself with the surface at hand. One pass is generally sufficient. Next, take the regular print brush that you use for black powder and, without loading it with fresh powder, lightly brush the same surface with the intent of brushing away the metallic flakes that are part of the magnetic powder mixture. The moment that you see any brush strokes or degradation of visible results, do not brush any further. Care must always be used at this step. Practice and experience will lead you to stopping just short of that result. Lift the result as you would any other latent print. This technique became a regular practice for me during my tenure.

This technique is also valuable if there is a significant time lag between the time the given surface has been disturbed by the perpetrator and the time the surface has reached you, whether it is the lab or the field. Degraded prints do not always allow for regular powder to adhere to them but magnetic powder, contrary to intuitive thinking, will often bring out those prints with significant contrast. The bottom line is that magnetic powder can be used for metallic surfaces, especially painted or enameled metal. I have also found it useful for ceramics where a regular brush may actually destroy the print in the act of development. Like any other new technique, I recommend practice on a nonessential surface area to gain mastery of the technique. Also, the first time you do it the darkness of the magnetic powder, as well as the volume, will be startling and you will be tempted to think that you have just made a major error. Finish the technique and you will see the value that this technique has for almost any field situation.

SITUATION 7—NIGHTTIME EVIDENCE SEARCH

Review of One Old Technique

In a perfect world, all searches for evidence would be done during a balmy day with clear weather and relaxed conditions. However, because we know that this is not the case (except on TV), we must make allowances for the insensitivity of our suspects when they choose to commit their crimes during that MOST inconvenient of times—the middle of the night. Having worked over 15 years of my career on the night shift and operating in a world of flashlights, street lights, and any light that is artificial, two techniques have come to my attention as being most helpful during those times when a given crime scene must be processed during conditions of darkness or, at best, minimal lighting.

The most glaring (pun intended) problem is that, of course, the world looks significantly different when viewed in artificial light at night. Hence, shell casings and other small items are often missed that may not turn up until a daylight search is conducted. Although the crime scene may be secured during that entire time it is still inconvenient and, of course, a potential opening for the defense to seek an explanation for the reason a given item of evidence was not located until hours later. It is always better to be able to say that all evidence was recovered at the time, even under such difficult conditions.

The first task is to define the nature of the problem. What are the specific conditions of artificial light in low light settings that make evidence harder to locate? The answer is found in the nature of the light source interacting with its surroundings. Practically speaking, the glare of an artificial light source tends to "wash out" or neutralize color and contrast because it is emitting light in a narrower wavelength than ordinary sunlight. Since artificial lights tend to be from one source (usually the flashlight in your hand), not only are the colors neutralized but the light source is unidirectional, creating a two-dimensional view in a three-dimensional world. Observe the example in Figure 2.9.

This problem is created by the standard police search technique of the light source (usually a powerful flashlight) held and rested on the shoulder and pointed downward at a sharp angle from the searcher as depicted in Figure 2.10.

This is, essentially, direct reflective lighting, which, under certain circumstances, is useful for

FIGURE 2.9 Object in artificial light (tungsten flashlight).

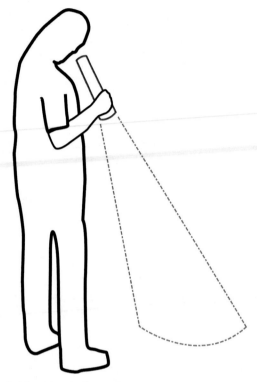

FIGURE 2.10 Depiction of common nighttime search technique. *Sean Miranda.*

photographing latent prints, but tends to be less helpful when searching for evidence. In latent print photography, colors and wavelengths can be appropriately filtered at the time of image capture and images can be processed to be sensitive to or filter out certain colors to make the latent visible and distinct. The use of specialized light sources can also give us helpful light wavelengths at the time of image capture. However, the eye sees everything in the visible spectrum at once and, therefore, the standard technique winds up creating our own glare with little or no contrast. In order to solve this problem, one must reduce glare and increase contrast, despite the limitations of using the same light source that is part of the problem.

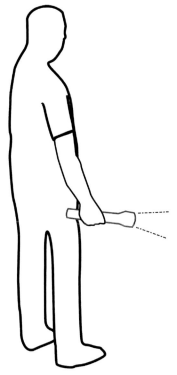

FIGURE 2.11   Demonstration graphic of oblique lighting position. *Sean Miranda.*

This is accomplished by a simple switch of light
source positioning. The light is applied in an oblique
manner by holding the light source down and slightly
away from the body and focusing the beam approximately 15–20 ft in front of the searcher (Figure 2.11).
Lighting further away is possible with experience, but
I have found that this distance is optimal.

By switching to this position, two things are accomplished at once. Glare is avoided against the viewer as the
light is angled off and away from the eye. Second, contrast is created by using the light angle to create shadows
of objects that are in place at the scene. The eye notes
the **contrast** that is created with a combination of light
source placement, light on the object, and the shadows

FIGURE 2.12 View of object using oblique lighting.

of said object produced by the light source positioning. The use of oblique lighting in the nighttime crime scene then simulates one significant aspect of the more natural view of the daytime scene. What is seen in a two-dimensional manner is now perceived in three dimensions, making the entire scene more familiar to perception, training, and experience. Figure 2.12 depicts the result of this technique and how the item would appear from the point of view of the searcher. Figure 2.13 is a close up view of the same item that shows the shadow created by this lighting technique. It is this shadow that creates the contrast needed in this type of situation.

This technique also allows the user to visually search an area significantly larger than the hot spot of a flashlight pointed at one's feet and with greater results. Thus, the Crime Scene Investigator's work product and efficiency are increased while simultaneously expending the same amount of energy and saving a great deal of effort and aggravation that is not uncommon at a nighttime crime scene. Although

FIGURE 2.13 Close-up view of object using oblique lighting.

oblique lighting is known in our crime scene investigation work it is not always used because the "shoulder" method is more natural. This also goes back to the previous section on intention. If we do not consciously choose, then we will choose a default out of habit. Choose the technique with intention then one will know one has chosen wisely.

SITUATION 8—NIGHTTIME EVIDENCE SEARCH

Introduction of a New Technique

The second technique addresses the unique problem of evidence in deep foliage such as a thick shrub or leafy bush in a nighttime situation. Once again, the standard technique is to have the light source (usually our flashlight) on the shoulder with the hot spot directly against the bush, as depicted in Figure 2.14.

Leaves can be highly reflective; thus, evidence is not located in a timely manner because the viewer

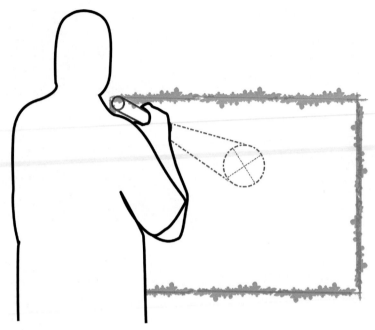

FIGURE 2.14 Depiction of common lighting method for dense shrubbery. *Sean Miranda.*

is creating his/her own problem. Many persons will aggressively shake the shrub or bush or strike it with a baton or other solid object in the hope that the evidence will fall to the ground; however, depending on the evidence, this can create a new set of problems. Further, officers who have seen an individual stuff or throw their little baggie of contraband into thick shrubbery and have then, subsequently, attempted to shake or strike the bush or shrub have revealed that such an aggressive technique can be unsuccessful in a significant number of attempts.

Through experience and experimentation, I discovered a more productive lighting technique for this situation, depicted in Figure 2.15. First, one picks a spot near the top of the shrub or bush and creates a "portal" into the bush, usually by using one's hands to spread

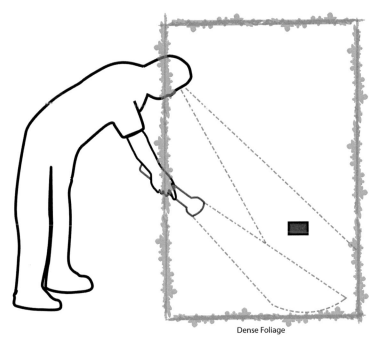

Dense Foliage

FIGURE 2.15 Graphic demonstrating alternative lighting technique for dense shrubbery. *Sean Miranda.*

apart the outer layer of leaves and twigs. Then, one places his/her face into this "portal," thereby allowing a view into the interior of the foliage. Finally, the light source is also stuck into the foliage at a comfortable position of the searcher's choice but, generally, at thigh level and aimed down at the base of the foliage, preferably the ground, as depicted in Figure 2.15.

While this position may be physically uncomfortable and, to some, a possible source of great humor, it has been field tested and proven to be an invaluable nighttime search tool for me and for the officers who have used it. To continue, the technique is completed by moving the light source in such a manner as to create background contrast from light reflected on the ground upward toward the viewer's eye position. Because the light is reflected, there will be little to no glare. There are other positions and directions for the light source that are useful from this position but I have found the preceding to produce the most optimal lighting.

Figure 2.16 is an ambient light photo of a handgun prop placed in a thick bush and the camera eye being placed in the same position as the viewer eye would be using this technique. A Streamlight 20L was used as the light source. The exposure matches what I saw with the naked eye.

It should also be noted that, although there are brighter light sources available these days, they have all produced a variation of the problems already discussed. Thus, a brighter and whiter light does not totally solve the problem. If one uses a light source that is brighter than the Streamlight 20L, a broadening of the beam should produce the desired result when applying this technique.

FIGURE 2.16 Close-up of prop in dense shrubbery using the Miranda technique.

As I know of no other who has advocated this technique, I am taking the audacious position of naming this the *Miranda technique*. It should be noted that, while the position is uncomfortable and I have had my share of spiders crawling across my face, the results in terms of locating evidence in a timely manner are well worth it. The first officer I know who attempted it admitted that his fellow officers laughed while he was performing the technique. He was attempting to locate a small bindle that a suspect he was chasing for a suspected drug violation had stuffed into the bush while running by it. The officers caught the suspect, but the bindle was needed as an element of the case. He noted that even the suspect had a bemused smile on his face. All laughter ceased when he successfully retrieved the very small object and the suspect, of course, had a moment of shock, being unable to comprehend how the object was located and retrieved. This indicates, by the way, the suspect's experience of success with this stashing technique and the realization that, perhaps, such success was now at risk. Whether the object is large like a firearm or smaller like a small baggie of contraband the technique, with some practice, is productive and useful in our never ending search for evidence.

SITUATION 9—EVIDENCE SEARCH INDOORS

When the Only Light Source Is Your Own Flashlight

Another very difficult evidence search situation is inside a darkened room with no ambient or artificial light immediately available. There are a variety of reasons that anyone searching for evidence may find him/herself in this situation, whether that person is an officer, forensic technician, criminalist, or supervisor. The reason does not matter, but when the lights go out at an indoor scene, it is not always prudent to wait for the mechanical/electrical issue to be resolved. It is, also, not always necessary with the proper lighting technique.

The majority of individuals in an evidence search situation will scan the light beam at varying speeds and at different angles using a direct lighting technique. This is successful often enough that it continues to be used and with decent success rates. However, the main danger of this approach is that the directional beam creates a series of stark shadows. Thus we strive to note each shadow and move the beam into that area so that we do not miss potential evidence. The problem is easy in an empty room or a room with very few items. However, if the scene includes numerous items of any significant size then the number of shadows compounds the problem, perhaps beyond our ability to keep track of them. Figure 2.17 illustrates that point.

An alternative approach is a bounce lighting technique in conjunction with the direct lighting technique. Do not abandon the direct lighting technique as that will still need to be used to confirm that whatever is first seen is, in fact, important to the investigation at hand. When entering the darkened room, point your flashlight straight up to the ceiling as if you were using an old fashioned torch. The stronger your light source the better this will work. The light will bounce off of the ceiling in an omnidirectional manner, dispersing throughout the room, and shadows will be at a minimum or even nonexistent. This dispersal of light will not impact your night vision as harshly as the direct lighting technique does and so that potential

FIGURE 2.17   Standard lighting technique, unlit and cluttered room.

evidence items will present themselves more readily. Figure 2.18 shows the same situation using the bounce lighting technique.

As your search yields potential items of evidence or interest, then a switch to the direct lighting technique is appropriate to fully determine the nature and value of the item in question. It should be noted that this technique is of no value for items underneath any furniture such as a bed or a dresser, so the direct lighting technique will still need to be employed in that particular situation. This technique is also effective in vehicle searches when it is necessary to search a vehicle before moving it from a scene. It is most effective when there are a large number of items piled on a given seat and it is necessary to go through them to determine evidence value. If there are very few or no items in that situation, the direct lighting technique will be sufficient. Let me emphasize that the bounce lighting technique

FIGURE 2.18 Bounce lighting technique, same room as Figure 2.17.

is ineffective as an evidence search tool unless used in conjunction with direct lighting. The trade-off is vision clarity due to eliminating encumbering shadows and light quality or intensity due to light dispersal. But use of bounce lighting will save significant time and energy that can be used more productively at another place or time in the investigation.

Chapter 3

Sequential Processing: Determining Evidence Value

Chapter Outline

ABSTRACT

This chapter expands the definition of *sequential processing* to include determining the relative evidence value at the scene. It explores the negative impact of the usual "take everything" method of evidence processing. Decisions made at the scene have short- and long-term impacts on the time, talent, and resources available for an investigation. We also define terms for discussion: probative, investigative, and others. We then use these terms to determine the known or deduced relative evidence value at the scene, relative to the decision-making process. Finally we present a crime scene graphic layout to see the concept in use as a tool.

KEYWORDS: Evidence evaluation; Investigative; Probative; Resource; Talent; Time.

Is it stuff or is it evidence?

There was a commercial in the 1970s by the Memorex corporation (a maker of recording tape before the advent of digital media) in which they showed a famous singer of the era hitting a note so high that it shattered a glass made of crystal (a feat that was demonstrated possible by a present-day *Mythbusters* television episode). Then, a recording of the singer's voice was played through the same speaker system, which again shattered the glass. The commercial concluded with the tagline and oft-used expression, "Is it real or is it Memorex?" with the idea being that one could not tell the difference. Many times, a similar situation can happen in crime scene work when it comes to determining whether the items found within that scene are evidence or not. The failure to recognize that difference can lead to hours of wasted effort. To address this issue, I am suggesting that a determination of the value of evidence be included in sequential processing.

The term *sequential processing* is normally associated with the application of chemical processes or physical means with the intention of producing useful results in the form of DNA, developed fingerprints, and so forth. However, the word *sequential* is from, of course, "sequence," which Merriam-Webster's dictionary defines as "the order in which things happen or should happen," and the word *process* is defined as "a series of actions that produce something or that lead to a particular result." Therefore, sequential processing begins at the crime scene with whatever actions are appropriate for the evidence at hand. Anything we do, including our decision-making process, evidence evaluation, and even note-taking for permanent documentation is part of processing. If the reader agrees that this argument is sound, then it can be understood that before any action is performed with regard to evidence, the first sequence of processing is an evaluation of that evidence to determine the ensuing appropriate sequence of steps.

When conducting an evidence search, regardless of the technique(s) employed or the number/skill level of the human resources employed, it is still necessary to evaluate the evidentiary value of the item. Although it may seem prudent to take the "better safe than sorry" approach and simply collect any and all items within a defined crime scene area, there are two main reasons to avoid this seemingly safe approach. First, such an approach unnecessarily expends available human resources. In addition, it invites a level of inquiry and attack in the courtroom that actually can work against the reputation of a department's professionalism and expertise.

Regarding the first point, I was taught in a class early in my career that all crime scene processing is a question of time, talent, and resources. The term "resources" does not simply mean the available equipment and funds, but the very real expendability of human resources. No amount of dedication, professionalism, personal toughness, or even the threat of discipline can stop a person from becoming more fatigued in the second half of a crime scene investigation than in the first half. Given that crime scene units in particular and police departments in general are experiencing diminished human resources, it is in the best interests of all concerned to use those limited (and, in some cases, shrinking) resources as wisely as possible. This requires planning and intention, with an eye for the best and most critical evidence with our first energy.

For the second point, taking every object in a crime scene to be evaluated at a later date may seem to save time at the front end of an investigation (by simply photographing, measuring, and packaging everything), but it adds time in the middle and the back end of an investigation. I will concede that, with modern equipment, digital photography and electronic measuring takes less time than it did before. Taking hundreds of photographs without the inconvenience of keeping track of numerous rolls of color negative film is a definite plus that I welcomed with the advent of digital technology. Also, being able to use the various electronic measuring devices is a definite step forward from the old days of tape measures and roll-a-tape. However, what does not change, no matter the medium, is that those evidence items need to be documented, whether on paper or paperless. Writing or typing still needs to be done for every item, and this takes time. I have heard many people say, "It just takes a couple of seconds to write in the form," but it has taken me 15 s to write this sentence. An honest appraisal will show that each item requires writing (in some form) on at least two documents, not to mention the cascade effect on anyone else who needs to document the item (e.g., detectives, property room).

After the evidence items have gone through not very many hands, those "few seconds" begin to add up. Then, the items need to be evaluated; invariably, there will be many "no, that's not evidence" items. All of that takes even more time, which has to come from *somewhere* or, to be more accurate, "some-when." Especially if it occurs at the station in follow-up mode, that time could be used instead on relevant evidence items. Furthermore, as the reader well knows, because all of this is discoverable, how does one explain under cross-examination the reason that "so many" items of nonevidence were recovered? Thanks to the media, rightly or wrongly, the jury pool is no longer impressed with a mass of collected evidence, but rather by relevant evidence that is discerned and recovered. Furthermore, tests may be ordered on the items determined to be not evidence, in the interests of "completeness"; in this case, what does one do with results that turn out be red herrings, wild goose chases, or any other favorite metaphor? This is beginning to look like a "hope for the best" approach.

A counterargument may be that we do not want to miss anything, I contend that if we take the time, at the scene, to evaluate the evidence with appropriate criteria, we will actually save time over the course of the investigation, recover all relevant evidence by exhibiting a quality investigation, *and* demonstrate superior professionalism. We can look the defense and the jury straight in the eyes and list out the rational and logical reasons why we did *not* collect something or disregard something. Juries can be trusted with this information—all of the information—if we give them the opportunity to make that assessment. We do not need to let fear rule our investigations; rather, we can use intellect and expertise.

So, how do we evaluate evidence? I suggest that evidence needs to be evaluated from two perspectives: legal and physical. I address and explain the physical perspective in the next chapter. For purposes of this discussion, I classify and define evidence categories as follows: probative, investigative, and other. The proper evaluation of evidence helps us to determine its degree of importance. Any item of evidence is technically of value, but I submit that it is not inappropriate to assign a degree of importance to a given item that determines how critical it is to a case, based upon the known facts of the case and any subsequent facts that come to light during the active investigation.

DEFINITIONS

As discussed in the introduction, the obvious cannot be overstated. As the reader is no doubt aware, *probative* means "to test or to try," with a second definition of "serving to prove"; such evidence is critical and important to the case at hand. Here, *investigative* refers to evidence used to search and learn the facts of the case, as part of a systematic inquiry leading to the identification of all participants. Such evidence has great importance, but it may not have the degree of criticality that probative evidence has. Evidence in the *other* category has two subclassifications: *stuff* and *anything*. *Stuff* refers to items that can either be seen at the time or through later investigation as merely property having little to no value whatsoever to the case. *Anything* refers to evidence that does not fit neatly into any other category but, regardless, serves to prove or disprove, support or refute, a possible reconstruction of the crime, the identities of the participants, or the possible activities of the crime. To be certain that the reader understands my meaning, I offer the following simplified layout of a crime scene (Figure 3.1), which details what evidence items belong in which category as they have been defined in this work.

In Figure 3.1, the location is a shooting in the middle of a four-way neighborhood intersection at midnight. The intersection has two streetlights that are on opposing corners, with one of them being nonfunctional (the compass direction will not be relevant for this example). There is a deceased victim in the middle of the intersection, with clothing that can be considered typical of one of the major gangs in your area (as determined by your department's respective gang experts). He has two gunshot

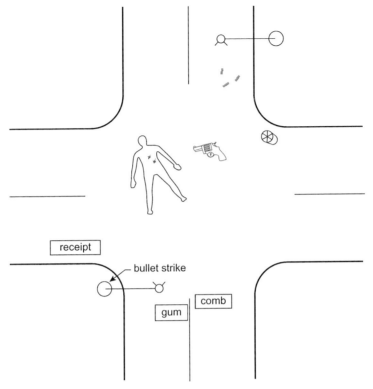

FIGURE 3.1   Crime scene layout (objects enlarged for clarity and discussion).

wounds to his center chest. There is a revolver on the ground next to his right hand. There are three expended 9-mm casings in the immediate area of the nonfunctioning streetlight. There is also a nondescript baseball cap on the ground, with hair in the headband. In the area of the functioning streetlight is a single bullet strike on the streetlight pole itself. On the ground, also in the area of the functioning streetlight, is a soiled and partly decomposed paper receipt for a local fast-food restaurant. In the same area, on the ground, is a hardened piece of gum squished flat, as well as a comb with a thick layer of caked dust or mud on it.

CRIME SCENE LAYOUT ANALYSIS

So, in the crime scene layout, which evidence is which category? Given the definitions already listed, the deceased victim and his gunshot wounds, the revolver, the bullet strike, and expended cartridges are all probative because they are the clearest evidence that a probable crime has occurred that resulted in death. (Some may say that it could be self-defense and the defender did not want to answer police questions; we will leave that theory as possible, but remote.) Subsequent investigations, specifically looking to see if the revolver has any rounds fired, could lead to the discovery of further probative evidence of an active gunfight that yields the potential of a second victim or a possible motive; again, these would be probative. Therefore, a shooting is our basic crime (depending upon the readers' respective relevant penal codes) and the aforementioned items are the items that are probative to that end. The street, victim's clothing, squashed gum, dirty comb, and receipt on the ground are not probative because none of those items are elements that prove a crime of any sort. One may argue for the value of the receipt, but we will get to that. The baseball cap on the ground, with hair in the headband and in the area of the expended cartridges, can be argued to be probative *and* investigative. First, the cap itself may have some identifying mark on the exterior or interior that may have some known symbology in the local area. The hair in the cap could, by DNA testing, yield the identity of the owner of the cap, a potential participant. If the hair is not viable, then the headband could be swabbed for DNA testing. Given this possibility and absent other immediate evidence, the cap is potentially probative because it could have been worn by a participant (shooter, victim, or witness).

Two items have not been accounted for in this evaluation. First is the nonfunctioning streetlight. This is not an item that can be collected because the streetlight is too big. Also, how does one collect darkness? This is an absurd thought, I concede, but it bears my point. It is still evidence, although of the documented kind (usually by photographs and notes) because, if the crime occurred at night, then the lighting conditions are potentially relevant. This evidence falls into the *other* category and the subcategory of *anything*, as described earlier. It has no investigative value but has probative value as to the conditions at the time of the crime; however, it clearly does not fit very neatly into a category despite its relevance.

The second item is the worn receipt. This type of item can be the focus of a great amount of misunderstanding and disagreement, so I devote a bit of discussion to it because it is central to my thesis of what is and is not evidence. Note that the receipt was described as worn and partially decomposed. What reasons do we have for considering that this item is neither probative *nor* investigative? The answer is its obvious age. One does not have to be a materials engineer or have any other training but common sense to know that paper takes more than a day to decompose and, therefore, the paper receipt has no value because it is not even from the day of the crime. However, many times, many crime scene investigators will engage in the conjecture of "maybe the suspect had it in his pocket and it dropped out when he got his gun" or a similar theory; thus, the aged receipt becomes declared evidence of probative and investigative value. From this, it may appear that we have left no evidence at the scene. However, I would argue that we have just stretched logic to its breaking point to the detriment of the case by a simple declaration based upon factors other than the logic of the crime scene.

If one sees an item that does not immediately fit into the flow of evidence and the current reconstruction of the crime scene, I would readily concede that such a condition does not mean that the item should be immediately disregarded. Equally, if one inserts it into the flow with a "maybe," absent logical cause, then this ought to ring warning bells for the investigation and thought process. Do we want to fit the item in because we can process it for prints and, therefore, obtain investigative evidence from it? This is a nonproductive mindset because it lays the groundwork for basing an investigation on what we can process and not on what is relevant. Are we afraid of answering the defense when asked, "Why didn't you collect that item of evidence?" We can tell the jury, face to face, that there was no logical reason because it was clearly worn and not from the timeframe of the crime scene; therefore, you did not collect that item because it was not evidence that was relevant to the scene. (More details on the court impact of this type of decision-making are provided in Chapter 10: Courtroom Techniques – Old and New).

Many investigators, even after agreeing with that these arguments are cogent and logical, may still want to collect such an item "just in case." For them, I only have two responses. First, just in case of what? Can you state your answer to "what" out loud so that it makes sense to others? The statement itself is not a reason but a preamble. If you cannot answer the question, then maybe it is because the answer has no logic and, therefore, the practice has no validity. If no cogent answer can be given but the practice is still followed because it makes one "feel safer," and you still cannot articulate the reason, then you are not engaging in forward thinking. This should serve to caution you as to what a jury will think of an investigative unit that operates out of feelings and fear rather than logic and good procedure. Second, if such an item is going to be recovered and processed, then you must remember that every decision at a crime scene has resource implications. Do you really want your crime laboratory to spend the hours it can take to process that worn receipt? If the answer is in the affirmative, then, at the very least, you are making an intentional decision that can be documented for further review. However, I would suggest that the use of resources that is driven by logic, good procedure, and protocol, along with the confidence borne of these factors, can only assist your investigations in a practical way as well as demonstrate an investigative unit that is not impacted by anything other than the evidence and the true direction of the investigation.

Therefore, despite the fact that the worn and partially decomposed paper receipt will be found in the photographs, we can confidently disregard it because the obvious impact of time on the item has clearly placed it outside the parameter of the crime and the crime scene. We would no more collect that item than we would the hardened gum or the mud-encrusted comb. As soon as we say "maybe," we need to call our own thought and logic process into question. All three items fall into the same category of *other* and subcategory of *stuff*.

When faced with any crime scene with physical evidence that needs to be collected for later processing to continue the investigation, the investigation is best served when logic is used and we place our feelings on a shelf. Is the evidence probative? Is it investigative? If it is other evidence, is it anything that helps us, or is it just stuff? Can we find the professional courage to call it that? I would submit that this approach is easily understood by juries and readily defensible under the most withering cross-examination. It also is the mark of a professional crime scene investigator looking to solve a crime who refuses to be sidetracked by anything other than good evidence and a logical crime scene reconstruction. This approach will make the best use of limited resources, both human and physical. Therefore, the first order of business in the sequential processing of a crime scene should be to determine if items are evidence or not. That may seem to end the discussion, but it is only part of the equation. Once physical evidence has been positively determined and identified, what do we do with it and when? This question is more important than it may seem, and it is the subject of the next chapter.

Chapter 4

Sequential Processing: Evaluating Evidence and Process

ABSTRACT

This chapter expands the concept of sequential processing introduced in Chapter 3 to include the physical evaluation of evidence. We first define the terms to be used, the fragility of the evidence and the destructive nature of the evidence processes used. We then explore how these terms can be combined to determine the relative fragility of a given evidence item. The evidence matrix is introduced as a conceptual framework that is flexible for any crime scene situation. A case study is presented to demonstrate the negative impact on time, talent, and resources when such a framework is not used.

KEYWORDS: Destructive nature of processes; Evidence fragility; Evidence matrix; Sequential processing.

The matrix of your evidence

This chapter presents the concept of an *evidence matrix*. Here, I am not using a popular motif to catch your eye (note that there is no capitalization and I do not have to pay anyone royalty rights). Rather, *matrix* refers to the Merriam-Webster definition: "something within or from which something else originates, develops, or takes form." What I propose in this chapter is not new; they are simple concepts put into an easy-to-remember format from which productive crime scene processing decisions can be made to maximize the resources that are available and ensure the maximum exploitation of all available evidence. When a scene has numerous items of evidence or requires a variety of experts that are not normally called into a scene, the one goal that everyone at the scene shares is to process the evidence completely, consistent with good and accepted protocols, and in a timely manner. However, many times a scene can seem so large in scope or complexity (or both) that, rather than taking 15 minutes of planning, we attack the scene immediately thinking there is no time to waste. Such an approach almost guarantees that a scene will take longer to process to the detriment of all concerned, including the investigation. The results could even be disastrous, with the best intentions being the cause.

DEFINITIONS

Two factors related to the documentation and recovery of physical evidence are the **fragility** of the evidence and the **destructive** nature of the processes/procedures used to recover it. I define **fragility** in two ways: (1) the physical nature of a given item and/or (2) the relationship between an evidence item and its surroundings. I also define **destructive** in two ways: (1) any process/procedure that has the potential to change the relationship of the evidence to its surroundings (including other evidence) and (2) any process/procedure that physically changes the evidence in any manner from its original state as found at the scene. Understanding the relationship between these two factors will help you to maximize the recovery of the evidence at a given scene.

APPLICATION OF THE CONCEPTS TO THE DECISION-MAKING PROCESS

The fragility of evidence can easily be misunderstood because it can often be linked to our perception of the importance of a given item or a plain lack of information or training in this area. When I have asked classes what evidence they consider most fragile, regardless of whether they are trained police professionals or students brand new to the profession, the most common answer has been "blood." When I ask the reason for that choice, I have usually heard some version of "it can dry up" or "you can get DNA from it." However, the former answer is not cognizant of the fact that DNA can be retrieved from dried blood and will not deteriorate over the time it takes to process a scene, even the largest ones. In fact, a viable DNA result was obtained from a blood stain recovered in the 1980s (thanks to forensic scientist Allison Flattum for this information). The latter response indicates that we are basing our answer on the process involved on this evidence rather than its actual fragility. Some classes have elicited an emotional response when told that "blood evidence can wait," which, after discussion, revealed a fear of losing evidence rather than a rational and logical evaluation of the physical properties of the evidence. So, in understanding this term and applying it to an investigation, it can sometimes be necessary to examine our own paradigms and let them go when the evidence calls for it.

An example of truly fragile evidence is a latent fingerprint on most any given surface. This can deteriorate over time, including quickly if the conditions are hostile to its existence, such as extreme heat or moisture, and any inadvertent action can wipe it away or distort it beyond its usefulness. A wet shoeprint on a hot day is even more fragile than that. A shoeprint impression in soft dirt or sand is another example of evidence that is fragile of its own nature; the soil condition (soft dirt in this example) is highly malleable and can quickly deteriorate over the time of an investigation. An example of nonfragile evidence is a bullet fragment with no identifying striations or a vehicle belonging to a witness of a crime. Although, perhaps, a caliber of weapon may be ascertained from the bullet, absent striations there is little else such an object can tell us; absent direct contact, it will not change over the time of a scene investigation. The victim's vehicle is important, of course, as to viewpoint; however, in and of itself, it is sturdy and there is no other relevant evidence unless one ascertains contact by a participant on the body of the vehicle. At times, a given item can be fragile and not fragile, such as a bloody knife on the ground or a suspect vehicle in the middle of the road. While there could be latent prints on either object, these objects themselves are fairly sturdy despite their probative importance and are, thus, not as fragile as the first items mentioned; however, fragile latent prints could be on either object. So when ascertaining the fragility of evidence, it is important to remember that the same item may fall under multiple categories of fragility, thus affecting the decision-making process.

To further complicate the decision-making process, the evidence item's surroundings can change how we categorize the fragility of the evidence. The same type of item can be fragile in one scene but not in another. A shoe impression in clay, for example, is not as fragile as one in soft dirt, even though it is still in the same classification of evidence. The shoe impression that is in soft dirt is, of course, fragile but becomes even more so if inclement weather is approaching and there is no ability to protect the item. A hair inside a quiet room is fragile but becomes even more so if that same hair is outside and the wind becomes a factor in displacing evidence items. Inclement or extreme weather of any type in an outdoor scene can completely change and even invert our evaluation of the fragility of evidence at a given scene. Therefore, the fragility of evidence is determined by a combination of its inherence nature and the conditions in which it is found, including its resting place and the surrounding conditions, whatever they may be.

Perhaps easier to note is the destructive nature of the processes and procedures at our disposal. The least destructive process that can be applied to any given scene is photography. Unless the evidence is sensitive to light in some manner (extremely rare but not impossible to imagine), photography changes nothing in a scene, while preserving the image of what was there at the time that it was discovered. An example of the most destructive process is that of physically recovering an item for packaging and transport. What is permanently lost is the item's physical relationship to the scene (although it is certainly digitally preserved). Another example of a destructive process is any presumptive test performed. Such tests consume evidence, albeit small amounts, but those amounts are consumed and permanently change the evidence tested. A presumptive test for blood may only require a swab, but that tested evidence is lost forever to the test and can never be recovered. We need to be aware of these factors when making decisions as to what evidence is processed, in what order, and what procedure is applied to the given item.

A framework of evaluation that assists in the maximization of limited resources, including time, will fill that need. In Chapter 3, we looked at physical evidence in light of its legal and investigative value and reiterated the high importance of such an evaluation. Of equal importance is weighing how long the evidence will be in physical existence until it is no longer recoverable. Evidence is not only legally important, it is also fragile. All of this decision making, while lengthy to read about, can be done with great rapidity and ease once the concepts are understood in relationship to each other.

Using the graph in Figure 4.1, the ideal sequence is to draw an arrow from the upper left corner, representing the starting point of a forensic investigation, to the lower right corner, representing the endpoint of a forensic investigation. All evidence is evaluated in the context of its fragility, understanding that an item may be inherently fragile or changing conditions can make it fragile. At the same time, we evaluate the processes/procedures either mandated or at our disposal. From this evaluation, a plan is formed that ensures the maximum possible recovery of evidence in the most professional manner that is helpful to and supports the investigation.

The following is an example of what happens when this approach is not followed.

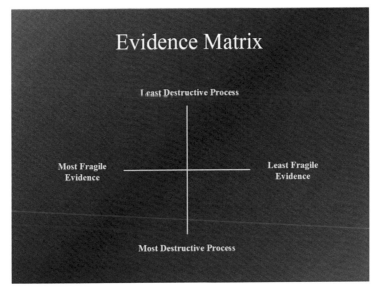

FIGURE 4.1 The evidence matrix.

CASE STUDY 1: A COLLISION OF RESOURCES

The scene was very high profile. A series of mysterious but horrific phone calls by a perpetrator led to the discovery of a horrendous scene. The female victim, in her own home, had been stabbed several dozen times, with clear evidence of extreme ferocity. Several different knives, all bloody, were found in various places of the house. At some point, postmortem, the victim had been beheaded, and the head moved to the fireplace of the house and burned. There was writing on the wall above the fireplace in blood and marker, as well as several items not associated with a fireplace on the floor in front of it. Gravity blood drops were seen throughout the house.

The only piece of news that had any sense of positive resolution was that the suspect was no longer at large and, in fact, was deceased (the details are not relevant). Given the extreme violence of the scene and its notoriety at the time, it was physically simple: blood in a variety of places, knives, a beheaded body, various items of various substrates that had every appearance of being moved by the perpetrator, and several areas with very personal items in terms of revealing the killer's mindset. These details dictated county protocols, which involved the necessity of a specialized callout from the coroner's office and it was also the desire of local authorities to request a blood specialist for collection and interpretation.

While the evidence was physically simple and the location was a tidy, medium-sized house, the evidence was all in small groupings such that the work of one expert was going to be on top of another, and each was going to require significant time for work. Without taking the 15 min for planning, all experts/teams were called in at the same time from separate offices throughout the county; they were not told of the tasks and needs of the others until all met at the scene. The initial response team actually began to do the work of one of the experts being called out (which was a normal part of their duties absent a callout), which led to the same evidence being processed by two different entities.

Although the teams were able to work out the confusion once they all met each other, each had to wait for the other to finish their respective tasks once a plan of attack had been reached. For reasons forced by the situation, items that had the potential for latent prints were the last to be addressed. One team of four had to wait 8 h before the way was cleared for its work, and the initial responding team of two had to stop their work for 3 h to wait for another team of two to begin and complete their work. An after-action analysis showed that by calling all experts/teams at once, approximately 38 man-hours were wasted. The initial response team could have completed the scene 4 h earlier without the necessary disruptions due to the resulting confusion. Fortunately, the case was closed, but who knows how this confusion would have played out in the public eye of a courtroom.

Case Study 1 Analysis

There was a need to document the body and evidence, recover and test blood from a variety of sites and items (including all knives), as well as recover items for processing for latent prints. The entire scene was inside a well-maintained residence and was out of the public view, thus greatly reducing the fragility of all items due to a stable and controlled environment. The most fragile items were possible latent prints on several items that had been determined to be of importance to the investigation. The blood, knives, and body were horrific, of course, but physically stable and considerably less fragile. Therefore, the body recovery team did not need to be called until well into the investigation, as the body needed to be photographed and measured, and blood needed to be tested and recovered. Several evidence items that were actually of greater fragility than the blood were in the way and could have been recovered prior to the arrival of the blood expert. The calling of the blood expert could have been coordinated with the initial response team, thus maximizing the work time for both and ensuring no unnecessary duplication of effort. The application of a rubric, such as the evidence matrix in Figure 4.1, would have been very beneficial in forming a plan, as discussed in Chapter 1. Such a plan would have prevented the stops and starts that ensued in the original case and would have been more helpful to the investigation, especially if it had been a case that had gone to trial.

Some may dismiss this case study as another example of "too many cooks" or even suggest that such occasions are rare. However, this scenario can often play out in a variety of crime scenes and, although the results may not be as dramatic, they can still be unnecessarily frustrating experiences despite everyone's best efforts to the contrary. Unless one refers to the involved experts, one is doomed to repeat mistakes. A former chief of mine once said, "The employee doing the job best knows what is needed to do that job." So, what is needed in a case like this? It is an understanding that sequential processing does not just involve what order to perform what physical process on an individual item that maximizes evidence recovery. It also includes the order to apply the forensic personnel for the same reason.

When evidence is being evaluated for processing and collection, a combination of the value of the evidence (probative, investigative, other) as well as the application of the evidence matrix needs to be applied when making decisions. It may be necessary to process a stable item of high probative value before a fragile item of investigative value. These decisions are best made with intention and understanding in a calm and professional decision-making process. If we take the "15 minutes" to evaluate what we know and what we see, it is easier to make adjustments as new information comes to light, be it a statement from a witness or the physical discovery of a new item. In this type of approach, we are actually employing 20/20 hindsight before it actually becomes hindsight. We need to always remind ourselves that an ad-hoc approach only has the appearance of addressing the scene in a timely manner. It is quite often an approach that can lead to frustration, inefficiency, and even catastrophe.

Chapter 5

Sequential Processing: Crime Scene Briefing

Chapter Outline

ABSTRACT

Understanding the crime scene briefing is a critical component of sequential processing. The level of detail can have a direct impact on an investigation. In this chapter, a case study is presented to demonstrate a briefing that nearly led to an unnecessary waste of resources due to the lack of necessary detail. An additional case study demonstrates the concept of working productively. We also discuss how to deal with contamination and include this information in the briefing to the scene processor.

KEYWORDS: Crime scene briefing; Evidence contamination; Sequential processing.

The truth the whole truth…

This chapter is intended for first responders and anyone in charge of an investigation who wants to maximize the forensic personnel at their disposal, whether they are fellow officers or civilian specialists. The subject at hand is the crime scene briefing, which is always the springboard from which it is decided what areas will be processed and when. Few would argue with the philosophy of rendering a full crime scene briefing to all participants in an investigation, thus making it possible for parties to perform their respective tasks for the benefit of the investigation. Sometimes, though, good intentions can make it seem as if we are following this philosophy when we are, in fact, laying an unintentional roadblock to it. A crime scene that is generalized or lacking significant details can lead to a decision in which an entire scene is processed when, perhaps, such a task was unnecessary.

Now some may inquire, "What's the harm in dusting everything? That's the job, right?" Taken in isolation, the answers to those two questions are "None" and "Yes." However, those questions always need to be taken in the context of the case at hand. Therefore, the true answers become "Much" and "Yes, when there is clear opportunity to recover latent prints". So, it is a demonstrable fact that there is *no* opportunity for recovery of a given type of evidence, applying the procedure for that evidence does not help the investigation but simply wastes time, talent, and resources that could be better used to process and recover evidence that *is* actually helpful to the investigation. Any forensic procedure is useful for evidence recovery, but only if the evidence exists in the first place. The procedure, in and of itself, has no value to any investigation absent a viable opportunity to recover the object of the procedure.

CASE STUDY 1: THE VIDEO

A brazen armed robbery of a credit union occurred in the middle of the day. Witnesses at the time said a single perpetrator had rushed into the location, got up on the counter, went into the open vault, and came out with two sacks of cash. He reportedly went back over the counter and out the door. No shots were fired and no one was injured. As can be expected, the witnesses were rattled by the experience, and this was reflected in their collective inability to tell what the individual may have touched or whether he was wearing gloves—a set of facts important to the forensic person responding to the scene.

Fortunately for the case, there was active video surveillance that recorded the event, and a review of the footage was readily available at the scene. The investigating officer and the forensic expert viewed the tape, which showed two significant facts: (1) the subject was wearing cloth gloves, and (2) the subject did not touch anything with his hands, except for the bags of cash that he took with him. When he jumped up on the counter, it was in a single leap, including exiting with the cash. He entered the location after someone else opened the door and exited by pushing with his back. The forensic expert knew that the physical evidence was not going to include latent prints, but it would include a possible shoeprint on the counter, scent evidence, and possibly DNA samples from clothing contact on surfaces. When the arriving supervisor asked what the video showed the officer, in his earnestness to fully investigate the case, the officer said that the suspect had "touched everywhere, so everything is going to have to be dusted for prints." Fortunately for the investigation, the supervisor asked for confirmation, and the misimpression was corrected. It was detailed from the video what evidence could actually be expected from the scene. The shoeprint and DNA were recovered in a timely and complete manner, a copy of the video was recovered, and the investigation was complete. The credit union was able to enact their after-action procedures and the police could begin their follow-up investigation, both in a timely manner.

Case Study 1 Analysis

If the forensic expert had not seen the video directly, one has to wonder how much time, energy, and resources would have been wasted. Many times, with the intention and expectation of saving time at a given investigation, one team member may attempt to serve as the "eyes" for another. However, unless both have considerable experience in the same field, one cannot speak to the needs of the other. Detectives, because of their advanced training and additional duties, will almost always interview participants, even after an initial interview by first responders. This is not an issue of trust but a matter of what is best for the investigation. By the same token, forensic experts, as much as is possible, need such information as directly as possible, particularly in the area of video surveillance.

It has been said that victims are usually victimized twice or often three times—once by the suspect, a second time by the necessarily invasive nature of a criminal investigation, and third time by the necessity to relive the experience in the court system. In Case Study 1, because it was clear that there was no opportunity to recover latent prints, it was unnecessary to further victimize those involved by forcing them to endure the time such an investigation takes or clean up after a forensic investigation of dusting for prints—a process that leaves a residue that is necessary but very unpleasant to deal with. Furthermore, it takes time away from the recovery of real evidence, which was the possible DNA and the shoeprint. What reason is there to delay addressing the clear places of evidence

MIRANDA, DAVID M.

EVIDENCE FOUND: AN APPROACH TO CRIME SCENE
INVESTIGATION.
                            Paper   176 P.
LONDON: ELSEVIER ACADEMIC PRESS, 2015

GUIDEBOOK TO RECOGNISE AND EVALUATE PATTERNS IN
CRIME SCENE INVESTIGATIONS.

  ISBN 0128020660   **Library PO#** SLIP ORDERS
                                     List   59.95 USD
   6207 UNIV OF TEXAS/SAN ANTONIO   **Disc**   17.0%
   App. Date   8/26/15   CRJ.APR   6108-09 **Net**   49.76 USD

SUBJ: 1. CRIME SCENE SEARCHES. 2. CRIMINAL
INVESTIGATION.

CLASS HV8073   DEWEY# 363.252   LEVEL PROF

YBP Library Services

MIRANDA, DAVID M.

EVIDENCE FOUND: AN APPROACH TO CRIME SCENE
INVESTIGATION.
                            Paper   176 P.
LONDON: ELSEVIER ACADEMIC PRESS, 2015

GUIDEBOOK TO RECOGNISE AND EVALUATE PATTERNS IN
CRIME SCENE INVESTIGATIONS.

  ISBN 0128020660   **Library PO#** SLIP ORDERS
                                     List   59.95 USD
   6207 UNIV OF TEXAS/SAN ANTONIO   **Disc**   17.0%
   App. Date   8/26/15   CRJ.APR   6108-09 **Net**   49.76 USD

SUBJ: 1. CRIME SCENE SEARCHES. 2. CRIMINAL
INVESTIGATION.

CLASS HV8073   DEWEY# 363.252   LEVEL PROF

recovery in favor of what amounts to a demonstration of capability without clear objective, purpose, or promise of a useful result? If your agency has an unlimited supply of people and time, then this thesis can be disregarded. Absent that fact, it is in our collective best interest to use our investigative resources to maximum effectiveness, which is not the same thing as doing the maximum number of processes possible.

I will not suggest to the reader that the case study presented is a pervasive problem; however, under pressure, it occurs often enough to address the issue. There could be a weakness in our collective investigative culture in which we are thinking about the processes that are available to the investigation rather than those that, after evaluation, are actually needed in that investigation. Are we, at times, confusing the concept of a complete investigation with the idea of the number of things we can do in an investigation? If that is our approach, then we expose our investigation to chasing an evidence result that does not exist. Information given during a crime scene briefing needs to be not only timely but also complete and factual in all aspects.

Many investigators have needed information that was not given because the desire to have a certain item or area processed becomes of paramount and even exclusive importance. However, given the theses of Chapters 3 and 4, evidence that is probative or investigative may be overlooked and the overall scene may not be processed in a sequential matter. The consequences of such errors could very well be evidence that is lost and no longer recoverable. Therefore, not only is it important to evaluate the evidence for its value to the known facts of the case as well as its place in the sequential process, it is important that everyone involved—in particular, the expert doing the evidence recovery—be informed of all known facts, especially any recordings of the event. I offer the following case study as a positive example of this concept.

CASE STUDY 2: STEP BY STEP

The scene was a murder with curious circumstances. The victim had been shot in his small apartment late at night. However, if any neighbors heard anything, they were not saying anything. Almost as if out of a movie, there was water boiling on the stove, but no cups had been removed from the cupboard. A coffee table had been knocked over. The victim had been discovered because the door had been left ajar, most likely by the perpetrator, and a neighbor who had come home from a nightshift job happened to see the victim on the floor while walking by the apartment.

Upon the arrival of the forensic experts, the investigating officer pointed out that no one had stepped on the linoleum floor, and he had the presence of mind to prevent anyone from doing so until the arrival of the forensics team. There were papers and other items on the table in the kitchen that appeared to be in disarray, but first responders had refrained from contaminating the floor to go get them, knowing the experts were on the way so timeliness was not an issue. The officer's request was to process the floor first and photograph the table so that the items could be freely accessed and fully investigated. Even though the floor and any shoeprints on it were of high fragility and of potential investigative value (recovery of identifiable footwear), they would not necessarily be first on the overall list. Due to the potential nature of probative/investigative of the items on the table, it was a logical request, so the subsequent decision elevated its importance and it was the first thing done.

Due to this level of interaction, teamwork, and an application of all principles previously stated, it was not long before the items on the table were examined and useful information was obtained, which was highly valuable to the investigation. While the shoeprints recovered were of poor to moderate quality, this result does not negate the logic of the decision-making process. There was no way to know the quality of the recovered evidence, but there was reasonable expectation that such evidence existed and was recoverable for an appropriate evaluation.

Case Study 2 Analysis

The investigating officer made this sort of briefing and planning his usual practice with the forensic experts at his disposal. There had been similar situations in cases of less severity in which, with the best of intentions, other investigators had walked all over a floor but failed to brief the forensic experts of that fact, then proceeded to request that the floor be processed for shoeprints. This, invariably, led to hours of predictably wasted effort with no useful results or, worse, an incalculable number of results that had to be recovered and cataloged once the process had begun. This police professional chose a factually based approach that avoided those pitfalls and produced investigations that were forensically productive.

When Contamination Occurs

It is not a great issue to defend in court as the reason that an area was not processed due to intentional or inadvertent contamination. Many times, it may be necessary to contaminate a scene in the interests of the public good. The classic example is that of an officer driving his or her vehicle right up to a gunshot victim, with the result being the destruction of evidence along the path of the tires; however, this is completely justified because a life may be saved. There are other reasons to contaminate a scene that are not necessary to list here.

When contamination occurs, especially if it was inadvertent, it needs to be communicated to the personnel responsible for doing the job of evidence processing and recovery. Explaining inadvertent contamination in court is not as scary as it sounds if it is handled in a forthright and professional manner (refer to Chapter 10, Courtroom Techniques – Old and New for more details on this issue). With the prevalence of a camera in almost everyone's hand, it would not be inconceivable to have to defend the processing of a contaminated area when the contamination was revealed on YouTube. It is more defensible to have a logical and professional reason for exploiting more productive areas of the investigation. Explain the factual and logical reasons for the contamination in a forthright and direct manner, and any supervisor, court, jury, or any other thinking person will understand and concede the point.

It will not help your case to keep your forensic experts in the dark on any aspect of the crime scene briefing, especially if, due to a lack of knowledge, they engage in the processing of a nonproductive area. Generally, once a task or procedure is begun, it is necessary to complete it for a variety of professional and administrative reasons. Do we really want to explain why an area was started but not finished? Do we really want to answer what was missing from the incomplete task when we can readily explain the reason the area was never processed to begin with? Do we want the court to see that an investigation was rife with a lack of communication and shared knowledge? Or, do we want to truly "cross the t's and dot the i's"? Understand that to truly do this requires total communication with everyone involved in the crime scene investigation, so thoughtful and logical decisions can be made regarding the best application of limited resources to a given investigation. It does not mean doing everything that is possible, just doing everything that is needed. The forensic expert needs the truth, the whole truth, and nothing but the truth. When possible, the forensic expert needs information as unfiltered as possible in order to apply his or her skills, training, and experience to the investigation. The court, the public, and anyone else watching will then understand that an investigation is professional, logical, and productive in every aspect.

Chapter 6

Evidence Processing: The Decision-Making Process

Chapter Outline

ABSTRACT

The need to ask the right question. Case study is used for entire chapter to explore the concept with a detailed analysis of the decision-making processes involved. Good decisions only come from asking the right question and recognizing our own presumptions. Presumptions, even due to good intentions, still cause problems in an investigation. A focus on a singular process can make the process the goal instead of a means to a goal. Striving for a systemic rather than a symptomatic approach to investigations which is about asking the right question.

KEYWORDS: Communication; Presumption; Researching evidence protocols; The right question.

Asking the right question of the right expert

Several years ago there was a very popular science fiction film in which a detective character was investigating a suspicious death. During the investigation he came in possession of a device that would play prerecorded messages of the dead character but the messages tended to repeat themselves or were nonresponsive. What the detective had to figure out was that it was, essentially, a video puzzle with a series of messages or information that would only be unlocked if he asked the right question. Many times, our crime investigations are stymied not by a lack of resource, training, ability, or even a lack of evidence, but the simple failure to ask the right question. The rest of this chapter will use the following Case Study as an example and for analysis of this concept.

CASE STUDY 1: A REQUEST FOR DNA

The Forensic desk received a call to have an expert accompany two detectives to assist in the collection phase of a search warrant that had just been approved. An expert was assigned and, upon contacting the detectives, was told that the collection would be for physical evidence and to bring their PE (physical evidence) kit. The expert asked, "What kind of evidence? What are we collecting?" The answer was, "Just bring your PE kit and you'll have everything you need." The expert took a regular PE kit which included items for dusting for latents, a small supply of items for immediate fluid collection, and a small assortment of tools, as well as a field camera. Further inquiry, prior to leaving the office, yielded the same "just bring your regular kit" response so the expert suggested that, as a precaution and not knowing what might turn up pursuant to the warrant search, one of the regular crime scene vehicles be taken as it holds additional equipment that may turn out to be of value. The response was "the warrant is for a specific item and you'll be riding with us, it's already been cleared." After the journey had begun the expert was informed that they would be meeting a suspect from an older murder case at the lawyer's office. Upon arrival into the parking lot of their destination, the expert was informed that the search warrant was for a specific number of hairs from the suspect's head, an equal number from each quadrant of the head (fore, aft, left, and right). Further discussion revealed that the goal was to obtain a DNA reference sample and that the detectives had done research that alerted them that DNA from hair was possible. The equipment items needed to collect such evidence were not a regular part of the PE kit that was carried by the forensic experts (sterile tweezers, etc.) so the expert was forced to improvise, borrowing items from the office and adapting items to achieve the goal of the specific number of hairs. The collection was successfully completed but it was an open question as to how this would play out in court or whether the evidence would be accepted because collection items could be said to have come from adapted common items rather than from department provided regular supplies maintained by the forensic unit. This was, of course, exacerbated by the fact that this had occurred in full view of the defense attorney in that very office.

An after-action analysis yielded the following issues that contributed to the situation:

1. An inappropriate presumption was made as to what is considered routine equipment carried by forensic experts,
2. Communication was fragmented and incomplete, even though everyone thought that they were, in fact, communicating,
3. The entire chain of events occurred because, in research for the search warrant, the right question was not asked and the right person was not consulted.

Presumption is the enemy of any good investigation. It is also the enemy of good teamwork. In this case, a presumption was made as to what forensic experts normally carried in their regular kit. Some may argue that the forensic expert should have anticipated every possibility and carried everything, but this is not logical or reasonable. In all aspects of police work, including forensics, there are specialized needs, units, and situations, otherwise one would need to have officers with 70 pound packs and an AR15 over their shoulders at all times to be "ready for everything." This is not reasonable, of course, and the same is true for all other specialized units, including forensics. Physical evidence kits are stocked according to the greatest need and, for most field units, it is for property crimes and the recovery of latent prints. It should also be noted that the forensic expert did recommend taking his own vehicle which would have had more specialized equipment, including for what was actually called for in the search warrant, but was overruled by supervision and absent additional information, had little to no reason to either protest the decision or expect that there would be a negative result. Some may argue that a supervisor's decision should be questioned if there is reason to question it, but that decision requires a reason which requires information. If that information is absent then the issue (in this case study) still centers on the original presumption of what a forensic expert normally needs in his/her PE kit.

In situations such as these, the temptation is to always look at what the other person could or should have done to question what turned out to be a negative idea. But a healthy, productive, and problem solving approach would be to examine how we got the idea in the beginning. In this case, the detectives rarely paid attention to what specific kit was being used when certain evidence was collected and they would have little to no reason to keep track of that. The job of a detective is hard enough without keeping track of every item of equipment that every employee, regardless of specialized unit, has at his/her disposal and it is not part of the job to do so. However, the job of everyone in police work is to avoid presumption. This is best done with good communication, which leads to the second finding in the analysis.

In retrospect, one might conclude that the detectives' response to the forensic expert's inquiry was negative in some way. Some may see condescension, a failure to listen, or even a disregard of the forensic expert as a fellow police professional. Some may suggest that a positive presumption is at work here, believing that any member of their forensic unit always has everything they need. Whether these aspects are true or not is a separate issue from this chapter and, in this context, are not relevant. What is relevant is that, for whatever reason, an inquiry was never fully answered and if it had been it would have spared all concerned any negative issue. The original questions of "What kind of evidence? What are we collecting?" needed to have been answered with the specific number of hairs required. The discussion, at this point, could have been over and the expert could bring the specific equipment needed, but, most likely, further inquiry would have ensued. "X hairs" from a crime scene or article from a crime scene is completely different from "X hairs" for a DNA reference sample. The first requires only collecting what is actually there, regardless of its state. The other has more specific recovery requirements for its usefulness to a criminal investigation to be valid. Many times, some have wanted to avoid such discussions with their respective forensic experts because they "...just want the evidence collected." However, full communication with one's own forensic experts will almost always yield valuable information and proper protocols applied as necessary so that evidence is not hastily or inappropriately recovered. Consulting the expert involved yields the best chance at viable evidence that, otherwise, could later be tossed out of court, considered unusable for analysis, or not consistent with testing protocols by the lab that does the testing and the evidence will, therefore, not be tested. In the case study at hand, "15 minutes of planning" and subsequent discussion would have made for a smooth recovery of the items sought. Finally, did the detectives want to avoid this discussion because they felt they had already gotten the forensic information they needed for their decision and subsequent search warrant? If so, this goes to the third finding and the next section.

The third and final finding was difficult for all concerned. In reviewing the case, the detectives knew that they had DNA evidence but lacked a DNA reference sample from the person they suspected. They began to look into various publications typically available as reference works for detectives, finding one that indicated that it was possible to obtain viable DNA from hair. One of the detectives proceeded to make contact with the FBI Crime Lab and asked, "Is it possible to get DNA from hair?" and the answer was, of course, "Yes." Then the next question was, "How many do I need?" and the answer was that the protocols (for that agency at the time) required 16, four each from the front, the back, and both sides of the head, and that each hair needed a root. This formed the basis for the very specific search warrant and, on the surface appears that due diligence was done. However, further analysis showed that, at the time of this case, the preferred method for reference DNA samples were buccal swabs, which are much easier to collect and yield an abundance of DNA without careful examination that collecting individual hairs required. Some may suggest that the FBI Crime Lab should have told the detective this, but the detective inquiry was about obtaining DNA and not about reference samples. The individual rendering assistance had no way of knowing this was the goal. It was also determined that the detectives' intent was to submit the samples to the local County Crime Lab, rather than the FBI Crime Lab, and the local Crime Lab's policy for reference samples was buccal swabs, which leads us to the second part of the third finding. For reasons that never became clear, the detectives never did ask the members of their own forensic unit, the forensic supervisor, or the local County Crime Lab. This was unhelpful, at best, since these are the persons that would be most involved in the collection. Further, it is in the interests of all personnel in the forensic community to maintain a working knowledge of best practices and general capabilities of specialized personnel so any failure to take advantage of that knowledge will rarely have a positive result. Although it may seem that obtaining an outside expert's opinion yields productive and unbiased results, this is only possible if one asks the right question. In this case, the question that needed to be asked was not, "Can you get DNA from hair?" because that is as much a crime scene question as a reference sample question. The right question would have been, "What is the best source of a DNA reference sample?"

Many times, in our collective desire to fully investigate all possible avenues of evidence with the goal of providing information that is useful and relevant we can wind up taking a symptomatic approach rather than a systematic one to questions. This can result in an unintentional but, nevertheless, a myopic approach in which we believe if we simply step up the pace we will reach the end of the process quicker to obtain the useful results we need for the case. Understanding this issue in our own decision-making process is especially important if one is seeking answers from a field in which we are not an expert. The best question is one in which we clearly state the end goal needed or hoped for but leaves the details of how to get there to the person from whom we are seeking information. The original question in the case study may have had this goal in mind but it was never explicit and focused on a specific process that was viable but not the most helpful. Essentially, the process (obtaining 16 hairs) became the goal (which was actually obtaining a DNA reference sample).

The question suggested at the end of the analysis (best source of DNA) had the end goal in mind and would have allowed the expert to give an answer that was the most beneficial to the investigation. Presumption can lead us to a false sense of comfort in which the truth of the matter occurs too late to be of use. Communication is a fundamental issue in any field of human endeavor including the teamwork needed if we expect our crime scene investigations to yield the best results possible. But even addressing the issues can be handcuffed into helplessness if we fail to ask the right question or mistakenly believe that we already have. It would not take much research to find cases that were stymied because investigators were convinced that they held the answer within their own knowledge and experience and the case suffered as a result. Ask the right question and one will not only get the right answer but, like the detective in the film, the right question will lead us to the right place (actual or metaphorical) in the investigation to ask the next "right question."

Chapter 7

The Schema of Criminal Investigations: Knowing and Not Knowing

ABSTRACT
Schema is defined and that we, in fact, have one. It is how we organize our experience into useful thought processes for an investigation. What do we do when we find something outside our experience? When do we consult experts and what are our criteria for choosing them? Two case studies are used to help answer the questions by redefining what constitutes an expert in a given field. The first case study demonstrates when we answer a question within our experience despite evidence that points outside of it. The second case study helps to define what constitutes an expert, especially in unusual circumstances.

KEYWORDS: Defining and using experts; Expanding scope of knowledge.

Be comfortable with what you know and what you don't know

Schema is an interesting word that one does not normally associate with crime scene investigations.

But it is one of the foundations of each criminal investigation, regardless of our role in it. Webster's dictionary defines schema as: "a mental codification of experience that includes a particular organized way of perceiving cognitively and responding to a complex situation or set of stimuli." In other words, we mentally organize our experience (mental codification) gained from previous investigations (organized way of perceiving cognitively) and use what we have learned to help us explain and investigate what we are seeing in the current investigation (responding to situation or stimuli). This process is, of course, what increases our skill level throughout our career. However, when we come across a "complex situation," i.e., crime scene, in which there are elements that are either unfamiliar or not fully explained by our previous experience, we need to be prepared to seek out new knowledge that may be beyond our experience, no matter how vast it may be. The mistake can come in the presumption that we have enough experience within the profession to overcome a lack of immediate knowledge in a given area. This is not always the case.

The question I pose is: At what point do we consult experts and what is our criteria for choosing them? This is not referring to experts with high expertise in areas such as blood spatter, trajectory determination, crime scene reconstruction, explosives, or arson. We know about those individuals from training, experience, or protocol. From time to time, however, the objects we collect or the situation of a given scene appears to be outside the knowledge and experience of the law enforcement professional. What we choose in those situations can go a long way toward whether a positive conclusion is reached in a timely manner or whether we remain in frustration because we are in a pointless investigative circle without realizing it. The following two case studies will help illustrate this concept.

CASE STUDY 1: UNDERSTANDING OUR OWN SCOPE OF KNOWLEDGE

Look carefully at the following photos.

The photos in Figures 7.1–7.3 are examples of evidence recovered from a series of burglary scenes that, initially, were quite baffling. The source of each piece is the coin slide/cashbox assembly to a coin-operated laundry machine which is of very heavy gauge steel. The incidents were occurring in the laundry rooms of apartment buildings of all sizes and in several different areas of the city. Further, the incidents appeared to be occurring at any given hour of the day or night and the damaged machines were always found by residents

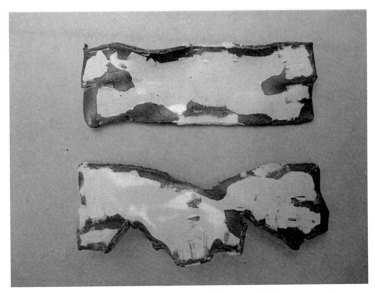

FIGURE 7.1 Typical pieces of heavy gauge enameled metal from scene.

FIGURE 7.2 Close up of single piece of heavy gauge enameled metal from scene.

FIGURE 7.3 Close up of edge of piece of heavy gauge enameled metal from scene.

who were attempting to do their laundry or, occasionally, by someone doing maintenance in the area. For several months, the coin slides and metal shrouds surrounding them were being forced opened in an unknown manner, exposing the interior cash boxes and allowing the numerous quarters inside to be taken. This left that part of the machine in a very damaged and unusable state. Despite best efforts on the part of the witnesses and the investigating officers, no one was ever able to recall anyone deemed suspicious and not a single usable latent print was ever recovered from any of the metal pieces or area obviously handled by the suspect. The loss from each machine was significant, especially when one considers the usual cost of doing coin operated laundry and how many residents there may be at a given location. It was the simplest case of "do the math," which the suspect obviously had done.

The cases continued even though, with each incident, officers flooded the area with as many personnel as could be brought to bear in hopes of identifying known persons or, at the very least, someone suspicious on any level, all to no avail. A sting operation was not possible, as there was no real pattern to identify, so the best hope was considered to be the ability of forensics to locate and recover evidence that identifies a suspect. Forensics suggested that perhaps the tool marks on the metal pieces may be helpful, even though there is no database of identifiable tool marks like there is with fingerprints.

CASE STUDY 1: RESEARCHING THE TOOL

Most of us have worked with a variety of tools and there was a collective attempt to ascertain what type of tool was making the marks found, repeatedly, on the metal pieces at all of the scenes. The majority consensus was that the tool was a vise grip. It was thought that, given the striations that were different from regular pliers and the need to apply great force in a small area, vise grips offered the best solution to the nature of the tool and the metal pieces were considered a dead end. However, this solution did not satisfy all of the physical dimensions of the tool marks and most dismissed this problem as one of distortion due the pressure involved in bending such metal. A minority consensus suggested that a hacksaw was involved but this had problems of timing since, in one event, a witness had taken their laundry to the laundry room and forgotten their soap. Reasoning that the retrieval of their soap could not have taken more than 5 min, this leaves little time for even the most expert user to do the damage necessary with a tool such as a hacksaw. As the reader can see, this was a point of great discussion in the case.

Two positive things occurred in the case. One was that Forensics, having the most access to the physical evidence, took the evidence to an appropriate expert. The other was that a young Patrol officer realized some very practical matters that had not been investigated.

Forensics took the metal pieces (the very ones in the previous photographs) to a local hardware store. It was decided to find a local hardware store that was privately owned, rather than a chain, reasoning that there would be individuals with years of continued experience with the development and usage of tools. It was briefly considered that the pieces should be taken to a mechanic, welder, or other tool user, but because it was uncertain what the tool really was, the deduction was that a tool source was a more viable option before exploring other avenues. The visit was met with positive results as experience verified deduction. Several individuals had been in the tool business for decades and upon viewing the physical piece took approximately 30 seconds to declare what tool was used, which they happen to normally carry. One of the pieces of metal that had been brought had an undamaged section and, upon producing the tool, the tool expert was invited by forensics to imprint a tool bite mark from the new tool onto the clean section. Figures 7.4–7.6 show the tool, the test mark, and a corresponding mark made by the suspect's tool.

The 2-foot channel lock tool (also known as plumber's pliers) met every criterion and, given its size, guided future responders to the areas of future scenes. Whoever was responsible had to be able to hide a tool this large in a way that no one was seeing. Although this still left significant room for conjecture as to how such a tool is hidden from view of witnesses, for the first time this conjecture would be guided by a solid foundation of logic and deduction. The individual could be hiding it in baggy clothing or could be carrying a basket of fake laundry large enough to

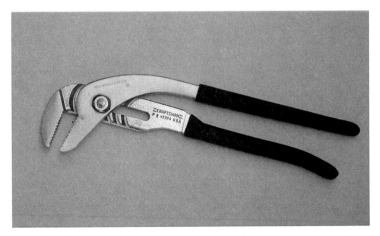

FIGURE 7.4   Typical plumber's pliers (aka "channel lock" pliers).

FIGURE 7.5   Close up of typical mark from crime scene tool.

FIGURE 7.6   Test mark from sample tool of same size.

contain such a tool while hiding it. Whatever manner was being used, and given that there are never enough resources to do everything we desire to do, such as stopping every single person on a block for a brief interview for information, this new finding made it easier for responders in future incidents to decide to bypass one candidate in favor of another.

CASE STUDY 1: RESEARCHING THE MONEY

The practical matter that had not been investigated is what was done with what were, certainly, the hundreds of quarters gained by the perpetrator? (This aspect is not necessarily a forensic one and is an avenue that could be pursued by anyone in law enforcement, although I would submit that it is more appropriate for those with powers of arrest.) Given the extremely large amount of quarters involved, the suspect had to do something with them given that buying anything in large amounts of coinage can draw unwanted attention not to mention the great inconvenience. A young patrol officer thought the matter through and while some suggested that the individual could have simply taken the quarters to a bank, the officer remembered from his training that almost all perpetrators desire anonymity and a bank is hardly the venue to maintain that desired goal. However, several stores in the area had machines that automatically counted coins and exchanged them for paper currency for a percentage of the input. He reasoned that anonymity in the use of these machines was plausible and that, given the quarters were stolen in the first place, a service charge was only the cost of "doing business." A visit to several stores yielded a very impressive result. At one store, several employees recalled that, for several weeks, the same individual had come in every two weeks or so and put numerous quarters into the machine, walking out with hundreds of dollars over the time period in question. Further, while no face was seen or could be recalled, they all remembered that he was a large man that wore an oversized green "Army" style jacket.

This gave responding officers all they needed since it was obvious where the tool was being hidden and, given the description, certain individuals could be bypassed if there were not enough resources to stop everyone for interview. The case ended with a positive result as an individual matching the description was found with numerous coins and the very type of tool that the tool expert said it would be.

Case Study 1 Analysis

What hampers investigative thinking is the thought that law enforcement has all of the resources necessary to solve any investigative issue. This simply is not true. Most would agree that, no matter what, our mutual goal is to resolve an investigation and put the appropriate parties in jail with any appropriate means at our disposal. It has been discussed in earlier chapters about presumption and one of the biggest errors that anyone can make, law enforcement or not, is that his/her particular life experience and knowledge are an adequate foundation for all situations and that all anomalies can be explained in the light of his/her own particular experience and knowledge. I would submit that if questions still persist and the current answers do not satisfy the facts at hand, then one must try a different course, perspective, or person.

Merriam-Webster's dictionary defines an expert as "having, involving, or displaying special skill or knowledge derived from training or experience." Many times, we may be tempted to believe that unless one has a degree or a certificate, one cannot be an expert. But if we keep an open mind, guided by the true definition of an "expert," we open up a criminal investigation to an almost endless supply of resources that can help us achieve a positive resolution to a crime scene investigation. All we have to do is be comfortable with what we know and be comfortable with what we don't know. We can always change the second through further study but at the time of a given criminal investigation, we are bound by the limits of our own history up to that moment, including our training, knowledge, and experience. The problem comes when we try to "reach into tomorrow" rather than admit we need help, especially from outside of the crime scene tape. When we do so, responsibly, we do nothing but further our cause.

CASE STUDY 2: REDEFINING WHAT MAKES AN EXPERT

An adolescent had killed him/herself by hanging. The methodology showed clear intent and a sad, but extraordinary commitment to ending his/her life. The individual had hung him/herself in such a way that all that was needed to save his/her life was to stand up. The hands were untied and there were no other restraints other than the one used to perform the action of hanging. An adolescent committing suicide is not unusual, of course, but it is still one of the saddest scenes that anyone, family or professional, could come across. If one has children of a similar age, the challenge is to put that emotionally and psychologically aside and focus on the facts and evidence of the case. Hard to do, of course, but it is our professional goal, all the same. What can add to the stress of a case are elements that appear to defy explanation or, worse, can seem to be indications of something far worse than what is initially presented by the evidence that is seen. Many are familiar with the various mass suicides that have occurred in recent history such as Jonestown in 1978 and the "Heaven's Gate" group in San Diego in 1997. One similar such incident had occurred within a short time of this case. Mass suicides are an assault on the senses of those who have to investigate them and a continual conundrum for those who examine them from a distance, including the law enforcement community. They are often couched in religious or other-worldly language and do not stand the test of outside logic but they still occur. In this case, a lengthy suicide note was found that detailed ideas that appeared to be of a religious nature, referring to a goddess and a prophecy and a number of other inexplicable things that had no reference point to any belief system known to the investigation team. The unique nature of the situation gave rise to the very real concern that this individual, given the obvious commitment to suicide and the apparent religious nature of it, may be part of a cult of some sort and this was the beginning of many potential victims.

The obvious focus, of course, was to determine known associates in the hopes of stopping further loss of life, if that were the case. One member of the team suggested that, as no one was familiar with the apparent belief systems being written, a copy of the letter should be shown to an expert in cults, if one could be found in a timely manner. This was agreed to be a potentially fruitful endeavor and as the team brainstormed for potential sources of information (the local seminary, a local popular priest, certain department members who had previous seminary training, etc.) one suggested a local game store where persons of all ages, particularly in the age range of the victim, would come for official and unofficial activities that were a part of this particular subculture. The team member suggested that, given the vast cross-section of clientele and the fact that what was written, if not out of the mainstream of known culture, was definitely out of the mainstream of police culture, that there was little to lose. (It should be noted that the age range for the location was preadolescent to retired and included scientists, musicians, artists, and a host of other unrelated occupations.) This was considered persuasive and a copy of the letter (with the specific portions detailing the specific desire for suicide redacted) was taken to the store owner who, upon perusing it, immediately called over two or three individuals who he believed would have useful input as the subject sounded like things they normally discuss. They were able to enlighten the investigation by pointing out that what had been written was a reference to a genre of animation that had not, yet, become popular in America but was very popular in other countries. Effectively, what had occurred was that the individual had personalized the characters and the stories in which they were involved and, while I will continue to acknowledge the very sad nature of the event, it was clear that there was only a very remote chance that a cult was involved. As one of the "experts" put it, "The creators of this genre had no more intention of creating a religion than George Lucas did when he created the Jedi, but people follow it and some even put 'Jedi' as their religion." The investigation team still conducted due diligence in contacting the adolescent's friends, winding up being the deliverers of sad news, but it was with the expectation that no other death situations would be found.

Case Study 2 Analysis

The individuals at the game store had no degrees, no certification, and had not gone to college on this subject, but by virtue of use of the knowledge and that, to some, they are on the "fringe" of "normal" society, they proved themselves a valuable asset due to the particular set of circumstances of this case. I'm certain that anyone would agree that research to broaden our own knowledge is part of any good investigation and professional endeavor. I would like to suggest that if we are open to what truly makes a given person an expert, we will be free to avail ourselves of an almost endless resource of individuals who, for whatever personal reason, have devoted portions of their lives to mastering skills or knowledge that we need from outside the walls of the police building. Remember that the dictionary defines an expert as "having, involving, or displaying special skill or knowledge derived from training or experience." Whether that someone has simply been selling tools for decades or is someone that seems to be on the fringe of society but, in reality, simply enjoys an unusual form of entertainment and recreation, our range of experts could be virtually endless.

In the aftermath of the previous case there was an unexpected side benefit in addition to the fundamental understanding of the case. This disparate group at the game store had the bragging rights that they assisted the police in a case. Did they catch a bad guy? No. Could we have found out the information given enough time? Yes. And were they ever used again? No. The store closed long ago and the group dispersed to other venues in the area, but what they carried was the story to their friends that the police needed them and they helped without hesitation. There is an old truth in sales that if one has a bad experience then 10 people are told and if they have a positive experience then three are told. At least for a while, with a very unusual (to many) group in society, a bridge was formed that no program, speech, or other formalized approach would have been able to bridge.

Chapter 8

The CSI Effect: A New Approach

Chapter Outline

ABSTRACT

An analysis of the phenomenon and the impact on the forensic field including an overview of TV entertainment, a discussion on what makes any show popular, and how that relates to the CSI (Crime Scene Investigator) shows. Five factors that the author feels have maintained the strength of the CSI viewing audience. The usual forensic industry response has been negative to the shows and the shows' fans. Our response should be positive, suggesting that this is related to sales concepts as the shows have made us salespersons of our work. Case study illustrating a different approach when faced with fans of the show.

KEYWORDS: CSI (Crime Scene Investigator) effect; CSI response to public; Entertainment.

You want us to do WHAT???

Before you give in to temptation and skip this chapter I ask for the reader's indulgence as I attempt what

I believe to be a different and, hopefully, more satisfying approach to this issue. I realize that the last thing we need is ANOTHER reason to hate all of those unrealistic forensic shows on TV and most readers will probably have had the "Yeah, I know there's an effect, I feel it every time I go to court" experience. We know that we are stuck with this state of affairs and I'm certain if I opened up a blog or other account I'd have no end of stories of citizens who "saw this on TV" and proceeded to get in our collective way. Worse, there is the high ranking police official who actually said to a Fingerprint Comparison Expert "Comparisons are all done by computer, aren't they? All you guys do is write the report and submit it, right?" and, yes, he was being dead serious. That type of a scene where the computer does all of the work is repeated in various shows where forensics play a part. I am certain that this and similar incidents have been experienced with many, if not most, members of the forensic community. These misimpressions are usually accompanied with an earnestness that fails to understand the frustration such a view causes. So I will readily agree that the popularity and pervasiveness of the CSI-related shows have had a negative impact on our profession. Now that the obvious has been overstated (an exception, perhaps?) here is where this chapter is really going.

ANALYSIS AND HISTORY OF THE PHENOMENON

While many shows occupy a nexus between reality and entertainment, police shows in general and forensic-centered shows in particular seem to be a unique phenomenon. The reason is that there is a potential impact on the real-world criminal justice system, from the crime scene to the courtroom. I will readily concede any real life accounts the reader may have confirming this and there have even been studies documenting this impact. And, generally, there is this feeling of helplessness, real or perceived, to change the situation and a resignation to live with it. I am suggesting that we may not have to do that if we can change our understanding of the situation and then alter our current approach to the matter. To do that we will need to delve into the history of television entertainment as well as the world of sales. This will not be exhaustive of either subject, of course, but will provide a framework for an approach to this issue that can return control of the perception of our chosen profession back to the hands in which it belongs, the experts themselves rather than the people portraying them.

One of the more significant areas of inquiry is to ask the reason(s) why the forensic shows are so popular. Many oversimplify that understanding by saying, "that's easy, money!" However, such a response refers to the reason that the shows stay on the air to begin with but the reason they are, in fact, making that money. If one looks at the history of television entertainment one sees some interesting things. First, it is easy to find the vast number of television shows that did not catch on over any given era. There have been numerous series with unaired episodes and premises that seemed good on paper but did not realize a fan base other than a devoted few. There have even been some shows whose short life span was extended by the fan base such as Jericho from 2006–2008 (an Internet organized fan response that resulted in tons of bags of nuts sent to the CBS offices until executives relented for a final season). There are numerous reasons and debates that certain shows were canceled, but one thing that is clear is that, by the cold hard fact of the viewing numbers, they simply did not make enough of the viewing public respond with enough interest to continue them. On the other hand, there are shows that have run a lengthy course. Television entertainment has seen several shows that were remarkable for their longevity such as Gunsmoke (20 years/635 episodes) and Bonanza (14 years/431 episodes), Dallas (357 episodes) that asked us "Who shot J.R.?" as well as M.A.S.H (255 episodes) in the 1970s, and Dynasty (222 episodes) in the 1980s. The 1990s saw JAG (257 episodes), the X-Files (222 episodes), and Everybody Loves Raymond (210 episodes) which began in that decade and ended in the next one. The present day entertainment landscape (the 2000s) has several shows that have displayed even more incredible staying power such as The Simpsons (on the air since 1990), the Law and Order series and spinoffs, and, of course, the CSI shows (all versions and titles). Also, of course, I cannot forget the old I Love Lucy shows (1950s) that are still popular to the present day audiences but never even surpassed the 200 show mark. History is undeniable in verifying the popularity of these and other shows of equal or greater numbers but not noted in this text. (My apologies if I've failed to give the reader's favorite show its due.)

So what does this mean? Entertainment executives have been struggling with that question since the beginning of the medium and careers have risen and fallen trying to answer that question. What patterns, if any, emerge for our present day understanding of the topic at hand? Some, perhaps, could be understood in the context of their time. However, it should be noted that the longevity of some shows has spanned two or more generations and others have found new audiences in syndication and cable, so this cannot be the total answer. It takes no special expertise to realize that every show in every era is about creating a viewing experience that connects with the audience and these respective shows all succeeded (or are currently succeeding) in doing that.

If we can distill the matter to its most basic premise it is that a long running and popular series gives the audience a viewing experience that has touched a certain aspect, a collective core issue, of that audience to the point where there is a great desire to repeat the experience. Some have given us incorruptible heroes, others allow us to laugh at ourselves, and still others explore the darker side of the human psyche, always a fascinating journey. No matter what the core issue may be, it is explored in a safe place, the comfort of our home and people we care about, and we want to repeat the experience because we always feel fulfilled in some manner at the end of the episode, otherwise, we would not keep watching.

So what do the CSI-related shows have that the audience wants to repeat?

First, there have been advances in entertainment technology as well as a change in the perception of the medium of television, which used to be considered the graveyard for yesterday's stars and writers. Today's shows are cinematic in quality, adding to the visceral experience.

Second, it is clear that the writers and actors want the audience to feel a "part of the club," OUR club. Now that is true, of course, for any show with a positive protagonist, but the CSI-related shows also add elements of many of the other popular shows. Each episode is, if well written, a good mystery which few people can resist. At the end of the show, the "bad guy" usually gets their comeuppance, the forensic equivalent of "in your face", and everyone can sleep safely tonight. That is the ultimate shared experience for both the viewing audience and the seasoned professional when the evidence, imagined (the shows) or real (our profession), leads to the incontrovertible and unassailable fact that an individual was involved in the investigation in question. Our thrill is different than what is portrayed, I agree, but the vicarious satisfaction for the audience is undeniable.

Third, since it is a viewing medium, the modern audience is not bogged down reading it.

Fourth, there is just enough truth to make the show work. Forensic Science is presented in a "wow" fashion that is occasionally accurate, compresses the real time and effort involved, and is, always, visually pleasing. Perhaps the role of science fiction films may have something to do with that and when people are telling us what we do is "cool" they are most likely thinking of some of the many visual depictions from one of the shows. If anything entices people to want to be part of the club, it may very well be this.

Fifth, the viewing audience can vicariously experience the best parts of our job without the "baggage" of reality that goes with it. As some colleagues have noted, the bodies don't stink and you get to break for lunch and always go home on time. Is it possible that the viewing audience is actually aware of this fact on some level, conscious or subconscious? This might explain the popularity of such shows that may be born out of a sense of respect or envy. I submit that this is the case as there is little else, in my view, to account for such continued popularity that impacts our profession on a case by case basis.

The five factors enumerated about the CSI-related shows make the viewing audience feel good about themselves so they want to repeat the experience. Given the times we are involved in with wars and an unstable economic landscape, people will grab at good news as often as they can, especially about themselves. Is it possible that the shows not only give all of the aspects listed but also make people feel smarter at the end of the episode? What else can explain the continuous anecdotes in the profession about civilians and untrained police professionals actually believing they understand so many aspects of the profession? Yet that understanding continues to be faulty and I find that all evidence, circumstantial as it is, points to these shows. If I am correct, who does not want to feel smarter at the end of an experience? We cannot blame the viewing audience for wanting these things but that means we are stuck with the public impact. So what do we do?

RESPONDING TO THE PHENOMENON

We begin with our own collective mindset. Can we admit that there are positive aspects to the show? I will restate my agreement at the beginning of this chapter that the shows have had a negative impact on our profession, experienced in different ways for each of us, but negative all the same. However, one positive aspect is that, collectively, we now have a face rather than being a camera and fingerprint brush with arms and legs. For those of us who were in the profession before the advent of the shows, we toiled in relative obscurity. Since then, the public has become more attuned to and aware of forensic concepts and procedures than before the show started. And, like it or not, we are very popular. Certainly, at some point, the reader has revealed his/her profession at a social gathering and became the sudden center of attention, welcome or not. I would argue that these are positives because of what we can do with these truths. Rather than wish the shows would stop giving disinformation and false expectations we can seize the opportunities they have presented whether we asked for them or not. In an article on this subject (June 5, 2005, Chicago Tribune), Ron Smith, Founder and President of Ron Smith and Associates, Inc., was quoted as saying, "We can't change what L.A. or Hollywood is doing with the shows, but we can stop trying to look at it as a negative. You're lucky you have a jury that wants to listen." So here is what I consider a more satisfying approach that has been field tested from the time after the shows came on the air and began to have their collective impact.

The most frequent response I am aware that forensic persons give when well-meaning (or not-so-well-meaning) persons bring up the CSI entertainment shows is "That's just a TV show" or some version of that. It is a response that, even when said in the most neutral manner possible, is deflating to the hearer. I call this "popping the balloon." Like a child with a balloon that they are having particular fun with at the moment, one's favorite entertainment show is similar in nature to the viewer. When one has a particular attachment to a series, regardless of the reasons for that attachment, any attack on the show is like the natural reaction a child would have if his/her balloon were popped by a complete stranger. We are strangers to the public even though we are public employees. The fact that "we're the police, so it's different" has no bearing if we have the temerity to "pop the balloon." It is imperative that we understand the need to become salespersons and teachers in each situation in which this issue may arise. Telling someone that it is merely entertainment is not an educational approach as it is highly likely that viewers are aware of this fact. It happens to be entertainment that makes them feel good about themselves and the usual approach, while personally satisfying, threatens to take that good feeling away.

RESPONDING: LET THE AIR OUT OF THE BALLOON BUT DON'T POP IT

What we can do, instead, is just let a little air out of the balloon. We know that "real life" is much more fascinating than "reel life" because we are in the middle of it and actual lives are impacted. Each time one of the shows is mentioned is an opportunity to teach and correct misimpressions and misunderstandings, and provide context. We can first acknowledge to the person that reel life certainly looks more exciting than real life and there is no harm in that. Remember, many of the public actually think we live those lives (which is the reason that we may be real popular at social gatherings right now). We can segue from the reel to the real by noting real results in real time from our own experience or from others. If we are good teachers (and most of us believe that we are), they will listen. We can skip the retort and go right to the teaching point. It still points out that it's just a TV show and we still have the satisfaction of correcting a misimpression or outright error in the shows but we do it without popping the balloon.

RESPONDING: QUESTIONS: A DISTRACTING OPPORTUNITY

Ever been in the middle of casework (field or lab) and someone (citizen or detective) comes up to you and says, "May I ask you something?" and you can tell that it may not have anything to do with the case at hand but a more general inquiry? Often, it seems that, after the experience, we want to ask ourselves whether the inquiry could have waited. A brushoff or even a polite rebuff may be tempting and even, at times, necessary, but unless there is a potential for actual grievous harm to the case (not including our patience), never say "No" to a request or inquiry. Such a question is another opportunity to "sell ourselves" and even promote the organization, which is always professionally desirable. It is another potentially positive addition to the framework that forms the perception of our profession, especially with the public.

RESPONDING: FORENSIC TRANSLATION

Remember to translate. Our profession can speak a particular language, just as any specialty of any profession does by nature and necessity. And, by all means, we do not need to avoid using the terminology that goes with the given subject as it is likely that there is an expectation that we do this on a normal basis, but don't forget to translate. We are not giving away any state secrets through translation and, while some may be impressed, there is an equal chance that many will perceive arrogance on our part if we do not. A refusal to translate implies that if the hearer does not know the meaning of the word they are not worth the time of an explanation. This is a variation of the balloon metaphor except, in this case, we're really saying "mine's bigger." Related to this is when someone uses a term that they learned from one of the entertainment shows. It is OK to be impressed as it does no harm to us, personally or professionally, and may wind up appropriately inflating the balloon that you have just let a little air out of. Some may object that this only encourages misperceptions and I will not argue against that particular point in this context. However, we do not have time to "fix" the matter and the shows are not going away. Is it not in our best collective interest to encourage in the correct direction, as much as it is in our power, and gain a positive view than be dismissive about the matter? In both cases, we can still attend to the work at hand, but one approach leaves us in a better state in the public eye with little to no cost to ourselves, for example, as in the following case study.

CASE STUDY 1: THE RECALCITRANT ASSISTANT

It was a "routine" burglary to an apartment in a moderate sized building (30 units). The responding officer had requested a forensic response and one was provided. The forensic technician arrived and walked up to the location with the usual camera and fingerprint kit. The responding officer gave a briefing to the technician about the known facts of the case and included a warning that the on-site apartment manager was being extremely "helpful," at the same time noting his right to be at the location as a vested interest (true) and the victim's unwillingness to ask him to leave (who asks their apartment manager to get out?). The manager had also not quite done enough that would have allowed the responding officer to legally eject him from the scene. As the technician approached the manager noticed and said in a very loud and excited voice, "Oh! Thank GOD you brought a fingerprint kit!" Avoiding the, admittedly, satisfying response of "What ELSE would I bring?" or something similar the technician proceeded to the apartment with the manager closely in tow. While assessing the scene the manager walked rapidly through the house pointing items of "obvious print value" that should be processed. He also made suggestions as to processes and even offered to assist. The technician remembered a colleague who, when faced with a similar situation had said, "You know, I don't remember seeing you in ANY of my forensic classes so why don't you step aside and let me do my job." A true statement, but definitely a popping of the balloon, if not shooting it right out of the sky! Instead, the technician responded to each thing the manager said with "Thank you," "I'll do that," or "That's a good idea," whichever was appropriate. The forensic technician rightly figured that there were more "thank you's" than there were new ideas from the manager which proved to be the case. During this entire time the technician was performing the forensic portion of the investigation. Finally, the manager asked if he should bring an object touched by the suspect from the back room to the front room to be processed. The technician said, "Don't you think I ought to photograph it in place first?" voicing the inquiry in a collegial manner. The manager was mildly embarrassed but was able to save face by saying, "You're right! Hey, I'll just get out of your way and you call me if you need me, OK?" The answer was, "I will do that, thank you."

Case Study 1 Analysis

The usual objection to the approach I've suggested to this issue is some version of "I don't have the time, I have cases to work," but I submit that if we do not take the time the long-term impact could be devastating to our business. The objections could continue, noting that police work is not a popularity contest and all that matters is doing the job and I will readily concede those and other related points as true in theory and in fact. However, what is also true is that the people who comprise our public are voters. In a time of relative economic stability in the early 2000s, voters in California rejected bond measures that would have either improved or built new crime lab facilities, something everyone agreed needed to be done, in principle. But voters would not willingly tax themselves to foot those bills, although other bond measures were passed in the same era. So one has to ask how the public can say "yes" to the need but not support the concept with their vote. A perusal of analyses as to the failure of these and other similar measures is interesting and insightful, but may not entirely explain the result as analysts were surprised at the results. Is it possible that these people were reacting to the "salesmanship" of forensic professionals who were saying "It's just a TV show?" I have conducted no study on the matter and have, at this time, only anecdotal evidence, but this analysis is based on a concept still taught in sales. If people have a negative sales experience, they will tell 10 people about it and when they have a positive one they will tell three people. Is it possible that, without meaning to, "NO" votes were created by popping the balloons? I cannot prove it but I have to wonder whether it is, somehow, related. There have been the juxtapositions of stated need but unwillingness to fund, which if that unwillingness were more pervasive, could be discounted as a general issue of the voting public. But it is not and I think that ought to give us pause to consider the theory proposed here.

Whether what has been suggested in the previous section is true or not, we can agree that the shows have made us salespersons for our profession and spokespersons for our individual units and we are stuck with that situation until the shows finally go off the air. With that in mind, we need to address the situation on our terms and for our benefit, when we can, hence the approach I have suggested here. Be teachers at each opportunity presented, embrace the fact that we are (now) salespersons of our profession, and remember to never pop the balloon, just let a little air out of it. I submit that with our intelligence, training, and experience, we are smarter and more patient than almost anyone. Let's use it. As stated before, the public will never forgive us for popping their balloon, but they will forgive us for letting a little air out of it. This approach should not be hard for people as smart as us.

Chapter 9

Emergencies: Plan, Respond, Create

Chapter Outline

ABSTRACT

Many emergencies are external but some are a direct result of a lack of planning. The need to deal with emergencies in a systematic rather than symptomatic manner. Plans need to include when money is scarce. Planning combined with actual committed dollars is true planning. Symptomatic approaches are avoided by writing down plans for foreseeable emergent situations or future needs. Case study illustrating what can happen when a need is foreseen and a plan is made, but at the decision-making moment the plan is not followed. Future needs are resolved by present day planning.

KEYWORDS: Defining emergencies; Equipment failure; Planning.

Choosing the nature of our emergencies

There are various types of emergencies that can present themselves to a given forensic unit. The obvious ones are the "now" events that require an immediate response by members of the unit. Other emergencies can be failed equipment of various sorts, budget issues, and human resource issues. Also, there is a unique type of emergency that is not as uncommon as we would prefer, which is the emergency that we create.

While there have been numerous written works covering the need for preparedness, never has that been a more appropriate topic than in today's world. It is certain that each reader has experienced the inconvenience that shrinking budgets have caused. The field of Forensics has always been given a high emotional and psychological priority and a very low budgetary one, which, history has shown, has been at the root of many emergent situations that have caused professional embarrassment to any given agency. Many years ago, during the early recovery from the recession of the 1990s a forensic unit, in dire need of updated equipment including replacement equipment, was told that the lingering economic effects of that recession prevented the approval of the valid requests. When it was pointed out that there were several funding sources, besides the general budget, that were being tapped for similar requests for other sections, the answer was that they would be "free and clear" to take care of those needs once "all of the sworn needs had been met." Perhaps the reader is already envisioning the argument of the undeniable relationship between anything accomplished in the forensic field and any and all "sworn needs." In other words, in the field of crime scene investigations there is no such division that is justified and a failure in any area is an invitation to consequences we would all prefer to avoid.

True planning for emergencies should include plans for when economic times are lean and there simply is no money for anyone. These plans also need to include what will be done in the times of recovery. Waiting until we get there only invites an emergent situation that was avoidable. The prime situation to avoid is to find your department in the news due to failures in a high-profile case, failures that are often caused by a failure to plan and commit precious funds before the need is emergent. Many forensic units have indicated that, when such warnings are given, the response is usually a "that won't happen" or "we won't let that happen" before the situation, in fact, happens. Planning combined with commitment to implementation, exhibited by the dollar amount actually committed or provided, is true planning. Anything else is strategic planning bordering on wishful thinking.

A plan, be it economic, tactical, or strategic in approach, helps us to respond when the emergencies, whatever they may be, actually happen. One of the biggest dangers is to allow one's vision to be overrun by the urgency of the emergency and lose sight of the future beyond the end of that emergency. This means, practically, that a failure to calmly create a plan designed for a given event or situation and implement it opens us up to the temptation to disregard those plans in favor of a "put out the fires" approach. At the end of the emergency the immediate result can feel like an accomplishment, but this is a symptomatic approach to a problem. We must certainly deal with the symptoms, but we must also remember that our response to an emergency should go to the core of the given situation and the symptoms can be a major distraction. A simple analogy is the difference between spraying water at the base of the fire rather than the fire itself. Too many times we are spraying the fire until we have expended the resource and, while the fire may eventually go out with this approach, many resources have been wasted, including time that could have been better spent elsewhere and human resources that may now be expended to the point of a safety issue. There is a reason firefighters, for example, look for the root of a fire and attack that or set back fires in certain situations so the large fire has nowhere to go. Our response to any given emergency must be needs based and not symptom based. If a plan was made, use it and do not let the urgency become a tyrant against good sense. Modify the plans made, if necessary, but don't disregard them because if they were good at the moment of calm they are, most likely, better than quick ones made under great stress.

If emergent plans have not been made, then make them. Each individual forensic unit has the best handle on what emergencies they are not prepared to face and for which ones they are prepared. When emergencies happen, whatever they may be, use or modify your existent responses. It is easier to modify a plan than to create one on the spot and you are more likely to deal with all issues that were a cause of the emergent situation and, subsequently, the symptoms that got our attention in the first place. If you have embraced this concept, it is my opinion that the reader, using your own training and experience in your particular situation, is best equipped to fill out the details that will follow. The purpose here is to warn of the pitfall that occurs time and time again. If for no other reason, plan and respond because you do not want your section to be either a negative news item or, worse, an object lesson. We want to be the ones who bring solutions to emergent situations, not the ones who create them. Having said the preceding, one of my proofreaders suggested that I give an example or two of emergent situations that can be avoided. I offer the following examples to jumpstart your thinking, if needed:

1. Many agencies use some form of electronic measuring device to map out crime scenes. If your agency is one of those, is there a plan in the event

of failure of all available devices? Accidents, inclement weather, or simple system failure can occur and a backup plan, whatever your agency chooses, can be easily implemented if it is already decided that information was disseminated.

2. If your agency uses specialists from a larger agency (i.e., ballistic experts, criminalists), is there a plan for when one is not available? The solution can be anything from freezing the scene (for days, if needed) until one becomes available, sending a member of the team to a class to obtain that particular expertise (and would that place that person on-call for that need at all times?), and taking copious photographs and measurements for later analysis? Each solution has its own set of related issues and viability but the important thing is to decide on one and implement it when and if it is needed.

The following case study illustrates when all three issues come together on one issue. One can see the need and develop a plan to meet that need. But a failure to respond to that need through plan implementation is what usually creates an emergency. At that point, the original plan is, more likely than not, inadequate to solve the new and greater problem.

CASE STUDY 1: THE NEED IS URGENT AND THE TIME IS NOW

The local police department had a forensic section that was, effectively, two tier in skill sets. Twenty-five percent of the section was trained for fingerprint comparison duty. This duty was compensated by a bonus but was an optional part of the job duties. Seventy-five percent of the section was ambivalent about the matter and the department had decided to avoid a potential labor relations quagmire and avoid changing the job requirements for present employees. As always, various situations changed the environment of this status quo so that the need for additional comparison experts was beginning to be felt. The department did not realize what was involved in training an individual to competency and requested a training proposal that would have brought the remaining members to competency in print comparisons. After considerable study and planning, it was determined that, if the individual member were allowed 6 h a week for training, they could complete training to competency in approximately 2 years. This meant that, for the needs of the sections that utilize forensic services, they would need to agree to give up those man-hours in order to accomplish the long-term goal. The math was simple. The section normally gave 320 man-hours a week in a 140-h workweek (two shifts with 4 h uncovered). This would be reduced to 284 man-hours a week to allow for 36 man-hours for training. High priority calls and other similar emergencies would, of course, be reasonable interruptions of the training schedule. The schedule would be set so that all affected personnel would know what human resources were available at any given time for planning purposes. Once completed, barring unforeseen issues, the department would have its entire forensic section trained to competency in fingerprint comparisons. For reasons that were never clear, this plan was turned down and it was suggested that individual members were "welcome" to train on their own time but it was felt that the man-hours could not be spared, regardless of the potential benefit. As the reader has surmised, no one availed themselves of the "invitation" to train on their own with no compensation. Two years later, due to a highly unique situation (the details are not

relevant), both examiners were unavailable for a significant period of time. The department was in dire
straits as there were several active field investigations
and court cases that suffered as a result. Upon return to
duty, the experts (who were also the trainers) were told
that they needed to have people trained in "30 days."
When told this was not possible unless the department
had the training resources and could give up the man-
hours for training, the department responded that this
was not possible and the employees had to "figure it
out." The department finally asked, "How can we get
the remaining members of the unit trained in fingerprint comparisons, RIGHT NOW?" The answer, of
course, is that such a thing is not possible.

Case Study 1 Analysis

The real solution to the above situation is in the uncomfortable truth that decisions made 2 years prior were
responsible for the creation of a foreseeable emergent
situation and that the only viable solution is to start
the clock, again, and proceed with the original training
course, knowing that it is STILL going to take 2 years.
We must accept the fact that, many times, no amount
of creativity, will power, expertise, or application of
human resource can fix an emergent situation that was
created by human decision. Nothing can replace the
time necessary for training to competency in any specialized field. This is not about respecting employees'
opinions or expertise, management competency, or
departmental commitment, direction, or intention, but
an issue of paradigm. Merriam-Webster's dictionary
defines "paradigm" as "a philosophical or theoreti-
cal framework of any kind." A thing can be true but
if it crosses what we *believe* to be true then we are

left with two choices: (1) we must either reexamine what we thought we knew to be true (our paradigm), or, (2) continue to believe our paradigm (for whatever reason) and disregard the thing that is factually true.

It is, hopefully, apparent that the framework or philosophy at work in the above case study is that some method exists to shorten 2 years of training into "right now" because of the need. But "need" does not change anything but the sense of urgency. We must always separate the need or end goal from the means or method it may take to reach that goal. If we make them one and the same then we run the risk of falling into the same trap and we may avoid, put off, or disregard a necessary decision until the negative impact of that decision is unavoidable. Success in the future begins in present day planning AND implementation. We can avoid the entire negative situation by simply accepting the paradigm that future emergent needs can only be solved by present day planning and implementation and that present day emergencies need to have already been planned. Does this sound familiar? It is a longer view of the earlier premise that "15 minutes of planning can save you hours of work," the paradigm suggested in earlier chapters for crime scene planning. Strategic planning calls for no less so we are not ruled by avoidable, foreseeable present day emergencies.

Chapter 10

Courtroom Techniques — Old and New

Chapter Outline

ABSTRACT

Court may be the least-favorite aspect of forensic work, but it also may be the place where it is the most known. Common and recurring questions and situations are discussed in this chapter, including the following: whether "yes" and "no" are sufficient answers, reviewing first impressions entering the courtroom, talking directly to the jury (or the judge), using language to demonstrate expertise then translating for the jury, an alternative approach to testifying to fingerprint identifications, and "100% certainty" in identifications. In addition, this chapter reviews our relationship with the defense and the prosecution; testifying to errors; and classifying them as clerical, procedural, or substantive. Following up Chapter 3, there is a discussion of justified but misunderstood decisions, evidence contamination, and hypotheticals.

KEYWORDS: Classifying errors; Comparison testimony; Contamination; Hypotheticals; Using technical language.

You want us to WHAT???

The courtroom may be the least favorite place for forensic experts to go. I am certain that there are many readers who will beg to differ, and I will admit that I always found satisfaction in meeting the challenges presented in this venue. As of this writing, I have never met anyone who enjoyed waiting in the halls for their turn to testify. To be fair, I also have not met anyone who did not enjoy the experience it included an opportunity to educate a jury at length on a given subject. I will readily concede, as well, that "enjoyment" or any other positive term may sound out of place, especially because our findings may deprive someone of some level of their freedom or even their life in a capital case. Let me assure the reader that it is not the intent of this chapter to provide tips, techniques, or secrets to finding professional satisfaction or enjoyment from the court proceedings in which they become involved. I am simply pointing out that, in general, it is one of the least favored aspects of the job (if we are honest with ourselves). I am also pointing out that it is the one area in which our work is truly known and where mistakes may be exposed, if any exist. It is also the one area of our work for which we seem to receive the least amount of training and direction. This chapter is not, of course, all inclusive. However, I hope to provide a foundation for better answers to questions and situations that are common, recurring, and, at times, uncomfortable.

ARE "YES" AND "NO" SUFFICIENT FOR TODAY?

Years ago, law enforcement witnesses were taught to answer "yes" or "no," provide minimal explanation, and always look directly at the attorney. Initially, this is how I was taught, and this is what has been seen from witnesses for a very long time. This approach worked in a different era and for a different society, but today's society and jury pool are populated with people who expect more. A review of a handful of televised trials in which it appeared that everyone but the jury pool saw the evidence shows us that either something is missing in our courtroom approach and demeanor or we did not really see what we thought we saw in the televised trial and known evidence. While the latter may or may not have factual validity, I believe our approach needs to change. Does the public expect a television *CSI*-type person? Probably. Is that us? In reality, no, but I am suggesting that we can meet that fantasy while maintaining our professional integrity and preserve the factual basis of any findings to which we are testifying. The first step is a simple change in our overall outlook, which, for some readers, may be a review or endorsement of what they are already doing.

PLANNING FOR THE FIRST IMPRESSION

We already know the overall basics of dressing professionally, preparation (know your report), and answering the question asked. The few classes there

are on this subject deal with these and related factors quite adequately, but a review of certain aspects
that can be forgotten in the stress of the moment
do bear repeating. First is our overall approach. It
is not inappropriate, as you approach the witness
stand, to have a professionally pleasant demeanor,
including a smile, and walk deliberately to the spot
where you will take the oath before you testify. Look
each juror in the eye, acknowledging their presence
whether they acknowledge yours or not. Some have
said, in objection, that this is "playing to the jury,"
and that the jury should only be concerned with our
testimony and the factual basis of it. I will not disagree with those thoughts; however, like it or not, it
appears that our entire courtroom proceedings are
"playing to the jury." Does it really put us above
everyone else if we do not do something as simple
as what has been suggested here? Or, perhaps, are
we giving the jury an initial opportunity to assess
us? This is, in fact, their job—to assess our truthfulness as well as the facts presented in our testimony.
We will present the facts, but does it really hurt to
give them a chance to look right into your eyes and
make an initial assessment of who they think you
are as a professional and a person? This period of
time, by the way, is the first impression. Do you
want the jury to see you as a professional machine
that can be characterized by the defense in ways you
cannot defend once you've left? Or, do you want
to give the jury an image of who you are as a person and a professional—one who is doing a job and
acknowledging theirs? I submit that, by this simple
action, you are communicating to the jury that, like
it or not, we all have a job to do and we are going
to do it together. If someone is going to negatively

characterize you after you are gone, they will have to work harder to do it.

WHO ARE YOU TALKING TO?

Once on the stand and a question is asked of you, respond to the jury as much as is practical. Remember, the old adage in law is that attorneys do not ask a question unless they already know the answer. It is the jury (or the judge, in a preliminary hearing) who needs to be informed, not the attorneys. There are, of course, rare exceptions, but we will not belabor those times because the situation and your experience can direct your actions at that point. Jurors will, more often than not, look like tennis spectators whose seats are at the net. So, answer while looking various jurors in the eye. This is very important when you are giving your voir dire because this is the opportunity for jurors to know the most about you as a professional. Eye contact will engage the jury while you talk about the numerous classes you have attended. If you have only been to a handful, either because you are early in your career or there is simply no training budget, then eye contact can help you emphasize the importance of each class you were able to take. For the uninitiated in courtroom proceedings, this will seem odd and, depending upon your personal background, can even feel rude. Attorneys understand this approach and expect it from trained professionals. A prosecutor caught me looking directly at him during an exchange of questions and answers, and I suddenly noticed that his eyes were directing me back to the jury as a reminder to answer them, not him. A defense attorney, quite savvy to this approach, asked for permission to approach and continued his cross-examination by interposing himself between me and the jury. I continued to make eye contact with those I could see and, once he saw that his actions were annoying the jury, decided to engage them himself during his cross-examination. Whatever the tactics employed during direct and cross-examination, answer the jury directly and engage them with eye contact, no matter how uncomfortable. For a short time, at least, the jury is part of the criminal justice team and deserves to be treated as such.

USE THE RIGHT WORDS AT THE RIGHT TIME

Use everyday analogies and metaphors whenever possible. The jury really does want to hear the proper terminology so they know that we know what we are talking about. They also want to know *what* we are talking about because they may not know, despite (or because of) the television shows mentioned in the previous chapter. Do the jurors know that *substrate* means the surface on which the print is deposited or touched? Do they know that *matrix* means what we used to develop it or make it visible? I recommend having a ready list of analogies, metaphors, and translations that are consistent with how you speak. In this way, you will accomplish the goal of displaying your professional knowledge in an appropriate manner while explaining what you are actually talking about, and you can do it without notes. This will enhance your credibility with the jury. You do not need to convince either attorney, only the jury and, at times, the judge. They are the only deciding factors in a courtroom.

PRINT COMPARISON TESTIMONY: AN ALTERNATIVE APPROACH

Related to analogies and metaphors, fingerprint comparison testimony has, at times, been a point of confusion and contention in the courtroom. I will not be dealing with any legal or scientific responses to Daubert issues that arise; there are already expert texts on this subject, and I encourage the reader to explore those. However, it is my belief that one of the many reasons this field has come under the various avenues of scrutiny and heavy cross-examination is that we may have failed to demystify the process for the jury and the judge. We can display a mastery of our craft and related scientific concepts, and we can be adept at addressing the legal challenges that are brought up. However, if we cannot get the judge and the jury to see through our eyes, we cannot expect them to understand the concepts of our world. The days are long past where we can simply point to our expertise, volume of training, and experience, and simply declare that our expertise is reason enough. Invariably the questions of "How do you do comparisons?" and "How many points does it take to make a match?" are asked, either by the prosecution or the defense, depending upon the courtroom strategy of each and any pretrial conferences you may have had. These avenues are usually explored by the defense to prove that comparisons are not a science but a guess. I recommend the following approach, which is an updated variation on a technique taught long ago by Pat Wertheim, CLPE (Certified Latent Print Examiner), who is well known in the forensic community:

First, ask permission to answer the question by using an analogy (I have never been refused this request). Then, tell the jury to imagine that they have been asked to compare a street map from a Garmin, iPhone, or Google Maps (it does not matter which one) with a satellite photo of their own hometown. Describe the process the average person would take by looking for shapes of streets, angles of intersections, and even shapes of buildings to see if those details are found in both mediums. It is very helpful if there is a very unique landmark in your area; for example, in Downtown Los Angeles, the Staples Center actually has the words *Staples Center* in large relief on the roof and is the only building in the world with this feature. What we are doing is describing the comparison process using something that the average person has, most likely, actually done or at least been aware of they can do in casual Internet usage. Relate the process to that medium, noting the use of two different views, a schematic map, and an actual image of the object, and note that after enough examination it can be determined that they are two different depictions of the same object. You can then note that if it is of their own hometown, such an examination would be very easy. Next, change the conditions, but not the medium or analogy, to any obscure town of your choice (preferably one without a significant known landmark) and note that such unfamiliarity will make the job harder. Then, one can ask the rhetorical question that is inevitably asked of the comparison expert, "How many details do you need before you can make the positive determination that both images are of the same object?" Now, you can point out that the first example is relevant when the details of a latent are so clear that it is that easy and that the other example is when the details are very difficult to determine. Note that, in both cases, there is no way to determine how many details are necessary to arrive at a conclusion, just as there is no way to say the number of points needed to arrive at a conclusion (go ahead and use the popular terms, or you will seem argumentative or arrogant). At this point, you can note that there is more to the latent comparison process than what has been described, but that this ought to give the court some idea as to how the process works and the reason that a specific number of points cannot be listed, although some do as a quality control.

100% CERTAINTY IN CONCLUSIONS

Related to comparison testimony, the issue of "100% certainty" of a conclusion is a common question amongst examiners. The Scientific Working Group on Friction Ridge Analysis, Study and Technology (SWGFAST), as of this writing, is recommending against the use of such absolute phrases. However, the phraseology has been used for decades and is not unknown to the general public. A National Academy of Sciences report from 2009 (a highly respected and reputable organization of distinguished scholars) has also complicated the situation by not only stating that such a finding is not scientifically plausible, but also suggesting that while there may be evidence to support such an assertion that did not mean that such a thing can be discerned. (A more detailed analysis of the report can be found in Chapter 11.) Finally, a number of examiners still use this phraseology and are convincing in doing so. There is no national consensus, although SWGFAST is attempting to provide a pathway for that consensus to occur. Absent this consensus or solid direction, I urge the reader to follow whatever their individual agency has decided with regard to this subject. If no decision has been made, then be aware that the concept will be brought up; if the "100% certainty" phraseology is avoided, you will need to have an explanation ready ahead of time for the reason you do not use that phrase. Because the justice system and the public are used to the idea, you will need to be patient and endure the doubts that will come from any professional refusal to accept the phrase or concept. If you decide to accept it and testify as such, you will need to have an answer that explains the reason you are not following the SWG-FAST-suggested guidelines. The fact that the guidelines are "suggested" provides a possible pathway of explanation here. Either decision has its own baggage and will continue to do so for the foreseeable future because, whatever we decide on this issue as a profession, we will need to explain the reason(s) we did not change things earlier. It is a fair question, and the criminal justice system and the people will deserve a fair answer.

DISCOMFORT AND BOREDOM: DO NOT SHOW THEM

Another issue is our general courtroom demeanor. If you are bored, do not show it. If you are uncomfortable for whatever reason, do your best to set that aside. (If your discomfort comes from a mistake made in your aspect of the investigation, we will deal that particular aspect later in this chapter.) During the David Westerfield trial in San Diego in 2002, the testimony of the various forensic experts was posted on various Web sites. One expert, during a momentary break in questioning, leaned back in the chair on the witness stand, allowed the shoulders to sag, and appeared to exhibit a clear "I do not want to be here" demeanor. While the trial led to a conviction and we have every reason to believe the evidence was solid, this was still an error to show a jury. The fact that it is obvious the individual's testimony was accepted ignores the fact that habits breed habits, and an unchallenged bad habit is very likely to be repeated. Whether our actions will be seen by the world or not, they will always be seen by the juror who needs the answers that only we have to our particular facet of the case. What reason do they have to listen if we exhibit boredom? What reason do they have to believe us if we display discomfort? What are we uncomfortable with?

PUBLIC SPEAKING: YOUR SECRET TERROR?

If the basic issue is one of public speaking, there are several resources that could be at your disposal. Is there a Toastmasters International chapter nearby (an organization that teaches public speaking)? Speech classes at the local community college? Does your forensic unit do moot court on an annual basis? This, by the way, is a great use of your volunteers if your department has a volunteer program of any type. Typical of many departments is to have a citizen's police academy that seeks to inform average citizens about the workings of a police department. Many use it to enhance community ties, and a useful by-product has been a pool of vetted individuals that can assist a department in nonemergent duties. Such graduates or volunteers are average people like your jury pool and can be an invaluable tool for ongoing training put on by your department or just your section. Will your department send you to a courtroom class? (Look for a class that has actual practice; many are simply lecture or discussion based, but nothing beats doing.) Any of the aforementioned approaches can help someone who has difficulty in public speaking and courtroom testimony. We have the resources—we simply need to commit and use them.

THE "OTHER" SIDE

The defense attorney is *not* the enemy. It is generally the older generation in law enforcement that was taught this and, in my view, it was wrong to do so. The view that we are allied with the prosecution against the defense still appears to be held by many, however. The defense attorney is not in the job of "getting their client off," although that may be the result. They are in the job of providing a vigorous defense, including finding and exposing our mistakes. Is it their job to make it look like we made mistakes, even if we did not make any? Yes, it is, and I would argue that is a legitimate goal on their part. I will concede that this view is a deviation from the dominant opinion in the law enforcement community, but it is nevertheless true.

Communication is part of our job. If we cannot communicate our findings through the morass of courtroom proceedings, then we need to gain the skills so we can. Use the various defense attorneys' tactics to improve yourself. I once told a defense attorney how grateful I was for her cross-examination because I found myself always mindful of her while working a scene. It made me better at my job. She exclaimed, "That is the *last* thing I want! My job is to make you look like a blithering idiot, not make you *better!*" I noticed the twinkle in her eye and could not resist a mild chuckle. We wound up beginning a professional friendship, but that never stopped her from trying *very* hard to make me look foolish, which I accepted as part of her job.

We do not need to fear the defense attorney, nor are they the enemy. In each case, they do not know if there was some malfeasance or gross mistake that has been either overlooked or covered up, and they are doing their job to try to find it, if it exists. For those who may express objection or outrage to this thought, thinking "I would *never* do such a thing," I would say, "How does the defense attorney know that?" Enough corruption, malfeasance, and gross mistakes have come to the public's attention in various ways, so we cannot say that it does not happen. We can only make certain that we, individually, are never guilty of it. But we are painted with the same brush, like it or not and fair or not, and the defense cannot assume we are ethical at all times. Their client's freedom or even life is at stake. The defense attorney is not the enemy and, at times, can be our best friend if we understand his or her approach. Let the defense attorneys make their attack and welcome it as part of the overall system; in this way, your integrity will shine that much more to the jury and the judge. If you fight the defense attorney and treat him or her like the enemy, you may give cause, without true cause, for the jury to doubt you when they should not.

THE PROSECUTION

What about the prosecution? They are friendly and we submit our work to them for prosecution, but never mistake that collegial relationship for friendship. The truth of the matter is that, in a court of law, we are a means to an end for all concerned. It is not the intention, here, to state or even insinuate that the prosecution wants to win its case at all costs. That is not true. Of course, one can find any number of articles to the contrary to point out the exceptions, but we are not concerned about those exceptions here. The prosecution wants to win its case fairly, but it wants to win. We are a means to that end and that, also, is part of the system we are all in.

Does that mean the prosecution wants to hide exculpatory evidence? No, but they will use us to emphasize evidence that makes their case, which also is their job.

Our job is to wade through all of these competing and necessary aspects of the criminal justice system and do our best to be a voice for that which has no voice— the physical objects that comprise the evidence at a given scene and whatever results that they produced. The best attorneys want to know the whole truth and will ask you for it or willingly listen when you offer it. The prosecution *can* be your best friend when you make a mistake, however.

TESTIFYING TO MISTAKES

You know it happened. A mistake was made, and you made it. Whether it was a clerical one, a procedural one, or a substantive one, there are few occurrences in our professional lives that can cause more anxiety than making a mistake that is going to be brought up in court. Are all errors the same? How do we deal with them when our turn on the stand finally comes? When faced with this situation, no matter the type of error or its impact on the case, it is best to request that the prosecution bring up the matter, boldly and even force-fully. Anything else looks like a potential cover-up. The defense is free to cover other areas and will inevi-tably ask the question, "What other mistakes have you made in this case?" However, you are on your most solid footing if an error is brought up as soon as pos-sible rather than wait for the defense to appear to have "discovered" it in court. Before this issue is further addressed, let us define these categories of error.

CLERICAL ERRORS

What is meant by a clerical error is one in which there is nothing more substantive than a mistaken entry on a form. For example, you have 100 pieces of evidence. However, somewhere on the evidence form, a number was listed twice and, somehow, you proceeded to finish your numbering incorrectly. This has happened to more people than perhaps may admit it. Is this the type of error in which the police are creating evidence or doing anything involving a subterfuge? No, of course not. However, it is an error and will have to be dealt with.

PROCEDURAL ERRORS

A procedural error may be a situation in which one skipped a sequence in processing evidence, but latent prints or DNA were still successfully obtained. This is, of course, more serious because a valid argument could be made that the skipped procedure may have obtained prints that could have generated additional information to the case. The procedure may have been temporarily forgotten, necessary supplies may not have been available, or there may have even been a good reason for the action. However, it will look like an error regardless, especially if your unit has detailed policies on how evidentiary procedures are to be accomplished. Generally, experience shows that a procedural error rarely hurts a case in terms of evidence lost, but we still must deal with the appearance of the error, regardless of the fact that there was likely no substantive effect.

SUBSTANTIVE ERRORS

Finally, a substantive error is one in which evidence is genuinely lost as the direct result of an error in judgment. A trainee, years ago, saw what looked to be a bloody fingerprint on a surface and immediately attempted to preserve it by lifting tape without any other processing. The reader's reaction ought to be predictable. A review of photos did not show whether there was any real ridge detail, so those involved will never know how egregious the error was, only that it was serious at the very least. Although a DNA swab was still possible, evidence was truly lost, which is the fundamental difference between a substantive error and a procedural one.

CLERICAL ERROR TESTIMONY

A clerical error is the easiest one to respond to, but it can be the one that can make us look the guiltiest of malfeasance. This may be because, after reviewing our case notes and discovering the issue, we can feel so foolish and are at a loss as to determine when the error was made or the reason that it occurred. It can be maddening and it can feel so shallow to simply say, "We're all human", even though that is most likely the very reason it occurred. When the prosecution brings up the issue, go right to the point, look into every juror's eyes who meet yours, and simply state without equivocation that the error was yours. It is not improper to express regret at the action. Some may wait until they are asked, but it is better to give that regret willingly and immediately, rather than wait for someone to ask you for it. Many will rightly point out that such a statement could be deemed as "nonresponsive" and could be stricken from the record. That is a judge's discretion; in the times I have known this to be used, no negative repercussions have occurred. The jury, your partner in the criminal justice system, will feel a bit wronged by the error. If you give an appropriate regret, they are more likely to move past it quickly, especially if it is, indeed, a clerical error. Once the error is freely admitted, your testimony is free to move to the other facts of the case.

PROCEDURAL ERROR TESTIMONY

A procedural error (as defined) can be harder to defend. First, you should know if it was an actual error in procedure, such that a step was neglected or forgotten, or if it appears that way due to a professional decision made at the time? If it is the latter case, then you must be prepared for rigorous cross-examination to explain our decision. Just remember to avoid, at all costs, any expression that sounds like the statement, "It was my decision to make, so I made it." It sounds heroic, but most jurors will take that as arrogance and an attempt to tell them to "just shut up and take my word for it." This type of statement has been made in court by professionals and is to be avoided, not just because it looks bad to a jury but because it is wrong in all aspects.

If you can justify a change in procedure, then you will be able to articulate the reasons for that change, especially to those outside of your field. If you cannot justify a change in established procedure, then you must admit that it was a procedural error and be prepared to say so, which leads us to the first aspect. Again, be sure to look at the jury. This situation will require more admission than is comfortable for the average professional.

In a major case, a forensic expert neglected to take enough photographs of a window that was a point of entry, taking only close-up photos of the marks made to force the window open—clearly a procedural error.

This made it difficult to give context to the close-up photos that came out in the trial. When asked if this was an error, the expert said right to the jury, "Yes, it was. And I cannot explain any reason I failed to take the appropriate photos, and truly wish I had that period of time back to do the job correctly." The jury's reaction was to bow their heads, with some shaking them, but clearly with regrets themselves. The prosecutor learned later that this turned out to be one of the biggest reasons they accepted the credibility of this witness, because of the willingness to testify to his or her own detriment. It is also possible that the jury could have used that open admission to disregard the rest of the testimony, but it is almost guaranteed that they will do that if it looks like the witness is hiding something.

WHEN TESTIMONY TRIES TO DEFLECT THE ERROR

Most experts will say that they are always prepared to admit any mistakes, but a look at transcripts or televised testimony may tell us otherwise. Years ago, a defense attorney was questioning a detective about a vehicle that was involved in an investigation. Photographs showed that there were coffee stains on the surface of the vehicle, and an inquiry was made as to the origin and possible significance of those stain. The answer was that, due to the high-profile nature of the case, there was a sudden rush of media into the area before police could gain total control of the scene. One of the members of the media put their coffee cup on the vehicle and another member bumped the vehicle, causing the cup to tip over and the stains to appear. The detective did a masterful job of maintaining that explanation in the face of withering cross-examination.

The problem with this answer is that a casual observance of a news field team will show that the camera person has their hands full with a 35- to 75-lb camera (depending on its age/technology) and the field reporter is holding a field microphone and a notepad (digital or manual). The only people who bring coffee into a crime scene investigation are the police. The author and the reader cannot be the only ones who know this or can deduce it. If that is the case, if even a single member of the jury knows or suspects this truth, then imagine the gross credibility issues that are now presented for the detective, the rest of the testimony, as well as fellow members of the investigation. It was clear that this answer lacked credibility, and the negative result from the jury endorses that theory.

One has to wonder what would have happened if the detective had instead said, "Yes, that was my coffee cup (or my partner's). It was one of the most foolish things I have ever done. I truly regret doing it (or allowing it), and I wish I had that moment back to have never done it." Two things would probably have occurred. Certainly, the detective would have been disciplined by their department. Also, although the professional's personal good sense would have been questioned, their credibility would be enhanced because the truth would have been told to the detective's disadvantage. If one is willing to do such a thing, the jury will get over the initial shock and disappointment and will, most likely, question many aspects of the police professional, even their character, but they can no longer question the credibility.

Attempts to steer away from an obvious truth may feel like we have "weathered the storm," but such actions only serve to make the job harder. If you find that you have made a substantive error, be prepared to admit to it as soon as possible. Many times, when such an error is made during the investigation, one is able to recover from the negative effects through various other techniques and procedures. The jury and the judge will be more likely to believe the negative substantive effects have been mitigated if you own the error to begin with. The obvious question from the defense would be, "What *other* errors/mistakes have you made?" The credible answer is (assuming you have told all of them), "No others that I am aware of." By continuing to acknowledge the error, this demonstrates your openness to other errors you have not discovered, while maintaining your credibility for the substantive facts of your work that need to get into the record and be understood by the jury.

SUBSTANTIVE ERROR TESTIMONY

No argument can be made for any positive outcome or possibility when a substantive error has been made. When is time to testify to the action and impact of such an error on the case, it is likely to hurt the case in some way. The only choice is to document the error when it is discovered to have occurred, understand the likely administrative consequences consistent with your agency's policies, and be prepared to admit the same openly in court and, again, directly to the jury. It is also likely that you will be asked the reason the error was made. Have an answer if you have been able to figure one out, or be prepared to admit that you have not yet ascertained the thought process that led to such an error. This will be the only thing that will salvage your credibility to any other testimony that you may offer. Jurors are more likely to believe someone who is willing to testify without hesitation against their own cause than one is who is forced to admit such uncomfortable truths. The jurors will be greatly pained, but they are less likely to disregard the rest of the case. Essentially, be prepared to openly throw yourself under the bus.

EXPLAINING JUSTIFIED BUT MISUNDERSTOOD DECISIONS

In Chapter 3, it was noted that some physical items can be determined to be simply a part of the scene and not a part of the crime. However, if they are in the photographs, it is fair to ask about the reason they were not collected. The key here is to maintain the terms and foundation of your forensic investigation, while not embracing those of either direct or cross-examination. Suppose you are asked, "Why did you not collect that piece of evidence?" This is typical of these types of questions and reveals a certain viewpoint of which we must be cognizant—primarily, the use of the word *evidence*, which is a powerful word packed with meaning. Most of us will go through cogent and well-thought-out explanations that will not be believed because we failed to deal with the most potent word of all. We can, instead, professionally reject the terms and bring the testimony back to the facts at hand, maintaining appropriate courtroom decorum. Some version of "I did not collect it because it was not evidence" or "I collected every item of evidence. That item was determined to be trash indigenous to the site" demonstrates respect for the question, provides a professional explanation to the jurors that speaks to your expertise, and takes away the foundation for the insinuation that you have failed in your job. If the item was not evidence (simple fact), you did not pick it up (another simple fact) and did not waste anybody's time with it (simple conclusion). The reader can adapt this to their particular venue and own personality, but the fundamental truth to this issue remains: You did not recover the "evidence" because it was *not* evidence; therefore, there was no need to recover something irrelevant to the case. Trust that the jury will understand this because they want to understand our work. We just need to give them the opportunities to do so.

TESTIFYING TO EVIDENCE CONTAMINATION

Evidence contamination is always a big issue in the courtroom, and it can be one of the most uncomfortable and inconvenient situations to testify to. First, if a contamination issue is not in a crime scene report or, at the very least, a side memo to the report, then it needs to be. Otherwise, we make it easy for the defense to claim that it "found" a mistake the police have made. Some would say that it is the defense's job to find mistakes; if they do not find the mistakes, then that is on them. However, this is not an approach that engenders trust with the public. Do not let the defense "find" it; give it to them openly in a report. A significant number of evidence contamination incidents have uncomfortable but rational explanations. Admitting the event and admitting the impact (contamination) builds the foundation for mitigating explanations, whatever they may be. Otherwise, we look like we are making excuses for something we claim we did not do.

HYPOTHETICALS: WHAT REALLY IS POSSIBLE?

Many times, especially during cross-examination, we are asked about possibilities in our evidence investigations. It can be a draining experience to continually address the hypothetical questions presented to us by the defense, and many witnesses have resorted to the ever-popular response, "Well, anything is possible." This used to be taught (and in some cases, still is) as a tactic designed to demonstrate that the defense is grasping for anything to "get their client off." Whether that is the true intent by the defense is not relevant here. The answer is usually an answer of surrender because we are tired of the wearisome questions. However, the problem is that the statement is false. Anything is *not* possible. Is it possible, under your own biological strength, unenhanced by anything, to stand where you are at and physically jump to the moon? No. This would be one of many questions with negative answers that would, in and of themselves, fill a book. This is important to realize because it is quite likely that at least one member of your jury realizes this and would interpret the comment as one of surrender or, worse, annoyance. Also, knowing that anything is *not* possible gives us the intellectual integrity and psychological strength to continue to point out, endlessly if necessary, the reasons that a possibility asserted by cross-examination is *not* possible. Many times, the attorneys themselves will say "Well, isn't anything possible?" In response, you can say with surety, "No, it is not." The reader may choose, at this point, to offer an example that is comfortable and consistent with one's own personality and style. By all means, remain respectful to the court and to counsel, but the fact of the matter is that "anything is possible" is not a true and factual statement.

This idea holds, although not as absolutely, if the word is changed from *possible* to *probable*. If you are comfortable in your findings to assign a probability and defend it, then do so without apology or regret.

If not, then respectfully decline, even if you must do so for what feels like 100 times. I spent three straight hours being given variations on the same hypothetical issue and for three straight hours answered, "I cannot answer that question because I do not have enough information to give an informed and professional opinion. It would be nothing more than a guess, which is inappropriate here." That was my same answer until the defense attorney finally moved on to something new. I have willingly answered hypotheticals before but, in this case, simply could not; it truly would have been a wild guess, nothing more, so I did not respond.

The truth is, anything is *not* possible, including many of the alternative theories to your findings suggested under hypothetical questioning. Never give up because, sooner or later, the judge will order the attorney to go to something new if the same ground is covered again and again. Some things may very well be probable, and it does not hurt us to embrace that truth. The truth shows that we are professional and not defensive, that we are advocates for the facts rather than a conviction (the jury's job). If a mistake has been made, by all means own it, address it, and expect that your credibility will be enhanced. A disappointed jury that believes you is more important than a jury that is impressed by your demeanor but doubtful of your truthfulness because it "just does not feel right." If no mistakes have been made (which is the usual case, in my opinion), then we do not need to give the defense the appearance of one that does not exist, nor do we need to cede ground that we have rightfully earned through hard work and the implementation of solid forensic procedure. The jury wants to hear and understand us and our work. That is their job, so we need to do everything to give them the chance to do so.

Chapter 11

Ongoing Challenges

ABSTRACT

This chapter addresses the 2009 National Academy of Sciences (NAS) report with regard to print comparisons without differentiating practice and practitioner. A process need not be quantifiable to be considered scientific. We must differentiate between being threatened by change and being cautious of it. This chapter examines comments made at the first public meeting of the National Commission on Forensic Science by Judge Harry T. Edwards, an author of the NAS Report. The discussion includes applied versus pure science, what we are and are not, and how this may have led to the NAS report in the first place. Finally, the chapter cautions about the real-world impact of current and future changes to small laboratories and units.

KEYWORDS: Applied versus pure science; Friction ridge analysis; NAS report; OSAC.

Are we a science?

As the reader most likely is aware, the now-famous National Academy of Sciences (NAS) report of 2009, *Strengthening Forensic Science in the United States: A Path Forward*, has become the foundation for the future of our profession. As of this writing, it is not only heavily influencing the future of our profession, but it has become the guiding document for the subsequent development of the National Commission on Forensic Science. That group had its first public meeting on February 3, 2014 and was addressed by The Honorable Harry T. Edwards, Senior Circuit Judge/DC and a member of the original NAS Report committee. His comments are pertinent to the issue at hand, and I will refer to them later in this chapter. His comments are quoted with permission and do not constitute an endorsement of this present work.

Although the NAS report and its ensuing impact may be a *fait accompli*, this chapter addresses certain issues of the report, while being mindful of present-day developments resulting from that report. Many other papers have presented excellent scientific analyses, endorsing or challenging the report's conclusions, and I do not believe I can do better in that particular area. I direct the reader to those efforts, beginning with position papers from the major forensic organizations, such as the International Association for Identification. My comments will be in keeping with the overall epistemological approach of this book, addressing what I see as the foundation of the NAS report as it relates to crime scene work and issues involving latent prints, from processing to comparison. This is not a dead issue. The National Commission on Forensic Science is initiating an Organization of Scientific Area Committees (OSAC) as part of the attempt to standardize forensic science practices and protocols, and that future work will trace its origin to the foundations laid by the NAS Report. Any work done by those committees will need to bear in mind the report and any errors in its analysis found in said report, if they exist.

Finally, this chapter examines some of the issues that may have led to the situation that invited such a study and report—issues that may still be having a negative impact as the National Commission on Forensic Science and OSAC move forward. Within the framework that has already been established and the direction already set, there may be a better solution to the situation than what the original report called for. We need to be certain that the path charted is truly forward and not simply more complex for its own sake. The NAS report has value—not simply because its authors are learned or experienced, but because there is actual truth in it. We can embrace the uncomfortable truths and assertively resist the errors in it, calling them what they are. Later in this chapter, I suggest reasons why we may have difficulty with that, and even how we got to this point in the history of forensic science.

First, let me acknowledge that the report did indeed examine issues in the profession and asked uncomfortable questions that needed to be addressed. I could probably sum up the analysis of the majority of specialties examined in the report with the question, "How do we know?" Of course, the report's analysis greatly develops that question. Essentially the single greatest viable issue the report brings up is: How do we know what we know about fingerprints, firearms, etc.? We need to be able to articulate the reasons we come to our conclusions, be they based upon statistical probabilities, known facts from the pure sciences, or applications from either of those fields. However, I also join with many in our profession in not considering the report as the last word or authority on the matter, although it has been made so from an administrative perspective.

At the time of its publication, the report took advantage of the presumption of authority it received—a presumption that I concede was not without cause. However, the report made certain presumptions of its own that are problematic. In the section entitled, *Summary Assessment of the Friction Ridge Analysis*, the report noted that members of the latent print community say that the analysis/comparison/evaluation-verification (ACE-V) method of fingerprint comparison has a zero-error rate if the method is followed correctly. The report called this position unrealistic and that it did not lead to a process of improvement of the method, insisting that the method and the user are linked and have many sources of error.

There were several significant problem areas in this analysis. First of all, a few examiners in significant positions of influence or authority in the community were allowed to make presentations to the authors of the NAS report in preparation for the report. However, it is known that they were not allowed the time to fully make their case for the zero-error rate of the ACE-V method, while others were allowed to make the case that supported the end result. If one looks at the literature, training classes, and presentations made at the various conferences, then the truth of the matter is that, at the time of the original writing of the NAS report, most in the latent print community subscribed to the concept that the ACE-V method has a zero-error rate and that errors can always be traced to errors on the part of the practitioner.

This leads us to the second problem area of the NAS authors' analysis: the conclusion (in the same aforementioned section) that the position of the latent print community concerning ACE-V methodology is unrealistic and fails to lead to a method improvement.

I am compelled to ask: What is the reason this assertion is unrealistic? There are no satisfactory answers given within the pages of the report, and its foundational assertions are accepted without question. The foundational assertion of this particular conclusion of the NAS report is the concept that the methodology of friction ridge analysis must be compared to other branches of forensic science that the committee has deemed properly scientific. I will not argue that DNA analysis (the NAS report favored discipline for comparison) shares more in common and is based upon standard practices of pure science laboratory analysis. That alone ought to have alerted the committee that they were attempting a classic "apples and oranges" approach and did not have the understanding of friction ridge analysis needed to fully demonstrate "a way forward".

Finally, the section in question made the error of attempting to call the methodology into question by mixing it with the practitioner, attempting to make them one and the same. The examples noted by the report were practitioner errors, not method errors. The method and practitioners are linked, for certain, but only in that the practitioner is compelled to use a method in order to perform an analysis, but the failure of one does not need to conclude the failure of the other. Their position also ignored the very real possibility that perhaps the method does not need improvement, only the practitioner. The method is like any tool, be it mechanical or systematic, which needs to be used properly. So, all "error rates," with regard to friction ridge analysis, are in the realm of the practitioner, not the methodology. Several learned papers have been published and excellent presentations have been made detailing excellent defenses of this concept.

The method and the practitioner, in any endeavor, are separate from one another. The NAS report has made the mistake of linking them to prove an already presumed thesis. How can it show us a way forward if it did not do a complete job of looking back at the true foundations of the discipline?

I would caution the reader away from the very cynical analyses offered by some experts in the forensic community that appear too simplistic in response, as they probably are. Let us differentiate between feeling threatened by change and being cautious about change. For example, in one presentation I attended, the presenter asserted that the reason we can reject the NAS comparison of friction ridge analysis with DNA analysis is that the latter (DNA analysis) only deals with "class characteristics." This, of course, is not true and would reasonably call into question anything else said by the presenter. A presenter in another session suggested that there is no need to question anything about friction ridge analysis because it has been accepted by the courts for over a century. Longevity does not equal truth; otherwise, I would point the reader to the infamous Dred Scott decision (US Supreme Court, 1857) that stated African Americans could not be American citizens. Just because it is law does not make it right, either philosophically, socially, or scientifically. In this way, the NAS Report is on good ground to question the forensic science disciplines. However, I would also caution those who wholeheartedly embrace the report in its entirety. The pedigree of any report is not, in and of itself, a reason to embrace it because it would not be the first time that experts missed key and relevant issues. In either case, dogma does not serve us. As we address the issues raised, either through our own voice or through leaders we elect in government or the private forensic organizations of which we are members, we need to truly ask ourselves how we got to this point in the history of forensics. Here, I offer one aspect of a possible answer.

REFLECTIONS ON THE FIRST PUBLIC MEETING OF THE NATIONAL COMMISSION ON FORENSIC SCIENCE

As noted earlier, The Honorable Harry T. Edwards, Senior Circuit Judge of the US Court of Appeals/District of Columbia and a member of the original NAS Report committee, addressed the first meeting of the National Commission on Forensic Science. In that address, he reviewed the findings of the NAS report, many of which ought to be cause for hope for our profession. He concluded with the view that the newly formed commission "...does not meet all of the criteria we had in mind, but it at least offers a measure of hope," acknowledging that the hope stems from the combined talent and wisdom of the members of that commission. But, in my view, the most revealing statement in his address was the assertion that the most significant thing the NAS report did was call for "real science" to support the forensic disciplines. He went on to detail court cases accepting forensic evidence without real science validating it, echoing the NAS report findings in the section of *Forensic Science Evidence in Litigation*. Noting the role of the Daubert decision (Daubert v. Merrell Dow Pharmaceuticals, Inc., 1993) in the discussion and reiterating the role of the judge as the gatekeeper of expert testimony, he makes a case for the failure of the adversarial system of the courts to act as an effective means of forcing the field of forensics to adhere to or be guided by true science as the NAS report defines it. As proof, he cited the NAS report findings of a lack of scientific research in the disciplines of "subjective matching" (which I take to be mainly about friction ridge analysis), including determining quantifiable measures of uncertainty and a continued call for scientific studies of the reliability of said disciplines.

With respect to friction ridge analysis, we know that the ACE-V method is not a quantifiable methodology. Does that make it unreliable or unscientific? This is not begging for any exceptions, but it is simply an insistence of having the discipline of friction ridge analysis assessed by relevant criteria, not assigned ones, which are not always one and the same. However, the NAS report, and His Honor in his remarks, both call for forensic examiners to own the limitations that do, in fact, exist in the discipline. This is uncomfortably true and we need to embrace that fact, collectively and individually. It does not do harm, even in court, to acknowledge this truth, as long as we have thought through and can reliably articulate the reason(s) it may not be true in the particular case at hand—that is, the process used overcame the acknowledged limitations of the discipline.

I am compelled to agree with His Honor that, to paraphrase, longevity of acceptance in the court is not a good-enough reason for continued acceptance in the court, although some individuals have made that a bedrock of their argument. Nor will I dispute the need for science in our work, from the crime scene to the laboratory to the court. However, I will maintain that "real science" has, in fact, found its way into the forensic field in areas besides DNA analysis. He quotes a well-respected legal scholar in the field of evidence, Prof. Jennifer Mnookin (UCLA, School of Law), that "science deals in probabilities, not certainty." Perhaps, the issue is rooted in the fact that we are not a hard or true science but an applied one.

APPLIED SCIENCE VERSUS PURE SCIENCE

When I first began my career in this field in the 1980s, it was heavily emphasized by certain instructors that forensics was an *applied* science. This is an important distinction that sets the field apart from any of the foundational or "pure" sciences, such as biology or chemistry. Merriam-Webster's dictionary defines our field as "relating to or dealing with the application of scientific knowledge to legal problems." Although this is old news, I am certain, to the reader, this concept has not been emphasized in recent years to the degree it used to be. Since the first Daubert challenge in 1999, forensic professionals have sought to make this field equal with all other sciences. The impact of our profession is great because it is in the field of criminal investigations, meaning that the current and future lives of many people are inevitably altered by the results of our work; forensics is no small part of that process. However, it seems that in our response to the pressure applied by the numerous Daubert and other challenges, we allied ourselves with the pure sciences. In this way, we may have made it easy for something like the NAS report to put on even more pressure, such that we have the appearance of "playing catch-up" to the rest of the scientific fields.

What if we had taken a different approach and said something audacious such as, "No, we are not a pure science. We are an applied science"? That would put us in the realm of the myriad fields of engineering, with which I suspect we have much more in common than with biologists, chemists, and physicists. Many of the solutions found in the various engineering fields have resulted from determining the certainties of the results of their research and the application of the appropriate sciences to real-world problems. I submit that friction ridge analysis is in that same class of problem/solution and, therefore, we can be certain of our results without probabilities. Engineering is defined, by Merriam-Webster's dictionary, as "the application of science and mathematics by which the properties of matter and the sources of energy in nature are made useful to people." The present state of affairs may have been inevitable, no matter which approach we took. However, I believe that a return to emphasizing that our profession is an applied science would help us. Perhaps in that light and from that foundation, we can be allowed to talk of certainties and not probabilities.

Certainly, there is the concern that a given defense attorney will note that we are not a "real" science. However, we can point out that we are not, in fact, a "real" science, just as the field of engineering shares that same status. The importance of our field is based upon what we do for the public, not what we are called. In that way, we share some models with the engineering field with our various certifications but, somehow, we have bifurcated our approach and seek to be in both worlds, the applied and the pure sciences. We cannot do that anymore than engineers can call themselves physicists. I think we would be best served by embracing the field of engineering as a model for certifications and standards of expertise and practice. In doing so, any attempts by outside agencies, reports, or government bodies to tell us how to do our jobs can be made moot. However, to do that, we must eventually agree upon some things.

The NAS report talks about national standards, and many in our profession have made attempts to point the profession in that direction. The main difficulty, as I see it, is that everyone wants to point to their own respective agencies as the leader. Is it possible that there is, in fact, more than one right way to do a given task? While many will disagree with another's basic approach, either on a personal or agency level, I have rarely seen one tell another that they are completely wrong. Is this professional courtesy or is there, in fact, more than one right way to do a given task? I would submit the latter, and that we can openly tell the public this fact and articulate the reason that it is acceptable in a criminal court finding. If it is not acceptable, then perhaps we need to admit that our collective approach has been in error for many years. Then, the questions arise as to who is going to fix the problem and who is going to set the standard. These are the questions that the National Commission on Forensic Science and the attendant OSAC will need to wrestle with.

A set of national standards may be inevitable. However, a significant factor must not be forgotten. The NAS report, particularly in its recommendations, appears to focus on solutions that only major laboratories will have the resources to fulfill. Whatever happens in the future as a result of this report, the results will have an impact on the smallest crime scene unit. It begs the question: What if changes are mandated that a small- or medium-size agency with a small forensic unit is not able to meet? Will that group be required to disband? Will their work and testimony be disallowed for failure to comply with these national standards? Will money be provided for all of these small groups—money that is in short supply to begin with for this field? Or, will forensics become the province of large agencies and, therefore, the volume of work available to the beat officer, the detective, and the public becomes something of past memory? It is for these reasons that you must make your voices heard. In my view, if the NAS report lacks anything significant, it is how their recommendations are to be played out at the smallest level. If we are going to be left with nothing but major laboratories, that will not serve the public. I urge the leaders of this movement toward standardization to remember that it is not the dozens or hundreds in federal, state, or large municipal agencies who will bear the brunt of the new tasks ahead, but the thousands in small and medium agencies. When the economy was flush, it was difficult for forensic units, large and small, to get funding. In the current economic environment, which looks to be very long lasting, dollars are even scarcer than before. Whatever the recommendations made at the national or state levels, it will take money for the thousands of smaller agencies to enact them, or they will be forced to disband because they cannot meet those standards. This, also, will not serve the public. Every forensic unit has a stake in this conversation, and we could easily be overlooked and even negatively impacted without our collective voice being heard. Let us be certain that the standards we make are not out of fear or because someone said we should do it a certain way, but that they are actually appropriate and necessary. Let us not be afraid to say when the standards we have are, in fact, sufficient for the task at hand and that there is more than one right way to do a task.

We need to feel free, as individuals and as a community, to alert the OSAC and the National Commission that any pending standards, protocols, strategies, standardized language, or recommendations ought not to be based upon an unquestioned acceptance of the NAS report with respect to friction ridge analysis, or any other specialty for that matter.

Chapter 12

Miscellany

Chapter Outline

ABSTRACT

This chapter provides a list of "do's" and "don'ts" for first responders. We address the issue of what to do when something that is needed simply is not possible. Additional tips and tricks for forensic practitioners are provided, include what to do when electronics fail; a method for the safe searching of clothing; and what to do when evidence is altered, moved, or destroyed.

KEYWORDS: Do's and don'ts; First responders; More tips and tricks.

Do's and Don'ts for First Responders and a few more tips

Although many of the previously discussed concepts could apply to areas of police work beyond crime scene investigations, this chapter is for the investigating officer, the detective, or the police supervisor who find that they need forensic services. Whether your forensic people are sworn or civilian, certain issues bear review before deciding what concepts to integrate, what you are already doing, and which simply do not apply.

While preparing for a presentation that was to be the forensic segment of a weeklong annual departmental training event, several officers suggested that I provide a "do's and don'ts" section and a "pet peeves" section in the presentation. They enlightened me to the fact that current police academy training does not contain the level of information about forensics as it did in the past. They speculated that it was not a question of interest but an issue of increased complexity of the law, and that time has to come from somewhere. Because the field of forensics continues to evolve into becoming a primarily civilian field, officers may have lost touch with knowledge about the field, what is available to them at a given investigation, and what to do and not do beyond common-sense knowledge. This chapter is a synopsis of that presentation, as well as other issues brought to my attention over the years that bear addressing.

DO'S AND DON'TS FOR FIRST RESPONDERS

"Do's" have been covered in detail in the earlier chapters of this work, and I will summarize them here:

- Be intentional in your application of a given procedure or technique, as well as the overall plan of action to process a given scene.
- Address evidence issues on the basis of their actual relevance to the case, as well as with a foundation of sequential processing. For example, recovering and immediately processing a firearm that is guarded by an officer rather than addressing evidence that might be rapidly disappearing, such as a wet shoeprint, is

out of that sequence. React not to what the physical object may represent (such as a firearm) but to its actual place in the evidence matrix.

- Do give a full crime scene briefing of all known facts of the case, not just the ones that some surmise may relate to forensics. A partial briefing is not helpful, does not save time, and can result in evidence being lost, regardless of the expertise of the forensic expert.

- Ask the right questions rather than the convenient ones. If you have a goal in mind and all questions are directed toward that goal, then the path of inquiry will most likely miss any viable alternates because of a failure to ask the right questions.

- Do remember to use the tried and true evidence of fingerprints. With all of the new technology emphasizing the use and power of DNA testing, basic fingerprinting has been known to get lost in the shuffle, sometimes to the point of not being done or requested (if an outside laboratory is being called in) if it appears that DNA is available to recover. DNA is powerful evidence; however, it does not tell us that someone necessarily touched something, only that someone may have touched, coughed on, sneezed on, etc., a given item. Fingerprints are only made if someone actually handles an item—a fact that is of positive probative value. Further DNA results, by necessity, take time. Fingerprint results are usually quicker and the database is larger. That may change over time, but that is the current situation and any change will not happen quickly. By all means, go for DNA but remember to seek out fingerprints at a crime scene. One does not replace the other; they are different forms that help the case in a particular way. (A final thanks to forensic scientist Allison Flattum for this section.)

- Finally, plan with intention and purpose for emergencies, respond to them when they occur, and do not create them.

Many "don'ts" have also been covered in detail in the earlier chapters, but here are a few additional ones that are worthy of mention but do not merit entire chapters.

- Do not point out where you "know" prints are located. Even a visible smudge does not always turn into a usable print after processing. It does not mean the forensic person did something wrong or missed something; it usually means it was never there to begin with.
- Do not engage in these types of conversations within earshot of the victim. It will create an unwarranted expectation that has no positive result. If you believe your forensic person is actually missing evidence, then address that upfront, in private, and away from the victim, with facts and tangible examples. If you cannot provide these facts and examples, then perhaps there is no problem and what was seen was simply a hoped-for result. Hope is fine, but we cannot let it graduate into a potential fact absent evidence.
- If you move evidence inadvertently before it is photographed, do *not* put it back. Even if your forensic person never knows about it, it is a bad idea on a number of levels. Laws against staging crime scenes are quite clear, and being in uniform does not make it an acceptable thing to do. Some may consider this action nothing more than correcting a police error, but it is technically staging. In the years before the ubiquitous use of cell phone cameras and widespread video surveillance that document our actions (intentionally and unintentionally), this was considered

a personal integrity issue—doing the right thing even if no one is watching. The assumption was that if such a thing was done, there was a just and reasonable explanation for the action. That argument may or may not have validity. However, in this day and age, do you really want to risk being on YouTube putting evidence in place? Would you accept that explanation if someone else did it, someone you do not know?

- There is no need to be specific about what forensic process to use in a given situation. Your forensic experts know how to address that issue. You may also end up asking for something completely opposite to what is actually needed. A supervisor at scene saw tire tracks that were of good detail and consistent with other evidence at the scene—ergo, quite possibly involved. He insisted on "one-to-one" photographs. When asked if he meant "scale" photographs, he angrily demanded "one-to-one" photographs and wanted them listed as such in the report. Because those are two entirely different techniques—one generally used for photographing fingerprints (and other equally small areas) and the other for later analysis and comparison of larger areas (such as tire tracks)—one can see the potential for confusion, at the very least. Simply point out that the tire tracks need to be documented due to their relevancy, and it will be done.

- Do not ask victims where the suspect touched. We do need to know that information, but this is a specific area within the "ask the right question" concept. Our victims want to help us. If we direct their minds in that manner, you will find that they are really translating that to mean "What can the forensic expert get prints from?", which is not helpful. Ask what was moved or what areas show activity. This prevents victims from trying to help us by overthinking the matter, especially if they happen to be distraught by the experience, and it directs their attention in a manner most helpful to us. It is also useful to ask if they have touched or handled any items left behind by suspect(s).

- Do not keep calling the forensics team back to a scene for "one more thing." This is usually done with the best of intentions, with the officer wanting to take as little of the forensic team's time as possible so they can move on to other obligations. The problem is that more time is wasted in driving back and forth for that "one more thing"—time that is completely unproductive—which impacts anyone depending on that forensic person's productivity. If you need your forensic person for an extended period of time, that is one of the things we are paid for. There is no productivity in driving, and each time you wind up waiting for the forensics person to get back. Finish the case and use your forensic person until you do not need him or her. It is possible that the continued presence of the forsensic person may assist in speeding up the overall time without sacrificing anything from the investigation. Time spent in assisting, evaluating, and thinking at a crime scene is far more productive than driving.

- When you are using a larger department for your forensic needs, do not expect that they will be available for you as soon as you need it. As we all know all too well, money is not endless and we are almost always compelled to make decisions based upon the funds available. For this reason, if for no other, many departments will find themselves in the position of depending upon a larger agency, usually the local sheriff's department crime laboratory, for their forensic needs. The urgency of one department's need must be weighed against another's, and limited resources, particularly human ones, are allocated accordingly. For example, at one point, the Los Angeles County Sheriff's Department Crime Laboratory was only able to field one firearms/ballistic expert on call at a time for any given 24-h period. This meant that first come was first served, and all others had to wait or deal with their situation a different way. I will concede the point that certain scenes, situations, and court cases generate a genuine emergent need that must be met in the most expedient manner and timeframe that is possible. However, many emergencies, as noted in an earlier chapter, are decision based rather than event based. As a result, many larger agencies that are in the position to assist smaller ones have found themselves to be the recipient of the oft-repeated phrase, "I needed it done yesterday," which is neither amusing nor helpful. This must be borne in mind to maintain a calm and professional outlook on the scene at hand, the case in question, and the forensic professional whose services you require as part of your investigation. It is not necessary to generate a false sense of urgency to "help get them going," but it is necessary to understand that, like it or not, your agency may very well be one of many. Understanding this assists in maintaining a professional and collegial atmosphere, which is a necessary component of any crime scene investigation. Army Rangers have a saying, "Slow is smooth and smooth is fast"—a maxim that applies in this area as well. If an individual agency finds this completely unacceptable, and that is understandable, then the agency needs to consider starting its own forensic unit. This would require an expenditure of funds and allocation of human resources, but it is the only viable alternative if an agency finds itself "one of many" but does not want to navigate that situation any further.

- Unless you are the direct supervisor who has the overall view of the workload of the forensic personnel under your command, do not volunteer forensic people for a task or a favor (especially to another agency) without checking with them as to whether they are, in fact, able to do that task or favor. Unless you are the boss, do not obligate them without directly knowing the impact of that involvement.

- Finally, do not make promises that a forensics person will need to keep, unless you are the one in charge of this person and know the impact of those promises. Many times, especially in interagency situations that are ad hoc, one agency has volunteered the services of its own forensic section so that, at the time, it has the appearance of interagency cooperation. The end result, however, is that a simple sentence or two winds up being a commitment in time and personnel that detracts from the home agency. Furthermore, this results in court time for the other agency, which continues to take even more time away from the home agency. Only the supervisor of a given unit truly knows what outside commitments can be reliably made while fulfilling the base mission and, presumably, that has been communicated to the people in their command. This concern cannot be brushed away with either "the forensic supervisor was not available" or "we are all trying to accomplish the same goal, put bad guys in jail." The few seconds it takes to make that assignment may obligate that person to days or weeks of commitment, during which they are not available to the home agency, which hurts cases. The direct supervisor will be the one who knows what is truly possible.

If We Say It Is Not Possible, We Mean It

This leads me to what can be a difficult area for some. We need to be able to admit when something is not possible. Many times, a forensic person may be asked to do something and be compelled, for various reasons, to regretfully respond that such a thing is not possible. Most will accept this, wishing the situation was different. But occasionally, focus can be lost and an individual may become myopic in a given idea and not be able to let it go. Avoid that situation by listening to your expert as to what is possible and what is not possible. Many investigators, in this type of situation, have responded with numerous alternatives, believing that the original request is indeed possible, even if it is not. Additional ideas and "new perspectives" are good catch phrases, but they are not always helpful in these situations. The forensic personnel at your disposal have nothing to gain by lying or avoiding a situation, and they are the ones who know best what is and is not possible. If something is not possible, additional orders or creative thinking does not make it possible.

ADDITIONAL TIPS AND TRICKS

When All Electronic Measuring Devices Fail

In Chapter 9, I discussed planning for emergencies. One of the examples I posed was what do we do if you have an electronic measuring device that fails. If indoors, most forensic units have steel tape as a backup, which will suffice for shorter distances. However, if you have a large street scene combined with catastrophic electronic failure and the roll-a-tape gears have finally seized (and that does happen), here is a handy backup. Once a year, use the functioning device to measure out 100′. Walk that measured distance twice while a colleague counts your steps. If you count them yourself, your gait can alter because of too much self-awareness of the process—something you may not be able to duplicate during an investigation. Simple math will give you the approximate length of your stride and a measurement that you can use with enough confidence to reliably write "approximately" in the report, with the knowledge that it is more than just a guess. In more than two decades of service, I have had to use this technique twice. Equipment does fail and money is not plentiful, but if I am at a scene I know I can walk it. Our stride changes over time for a variety of natural reasons, which is the reason I recommend measuring your stride yearly.

Another Method for Safe Searching of Clothing

When clothing has been left on the ground at a scene, either because the suspect discarded it or it was removed by paramedics (or any other reason), more often than not it must be collected as evidence for the case. What is often done is that it is simply rolled up as is and placed into an appropriate evidence bag, with inventory done later. At times, for tactical reasons, this needs to be done, and I acknowledge such exceptions. However, whenever possible, search this clothing at its place of collection. Lay the clothing out carefully and use the flat of your hand, gently, to feel the various areas of the clothing, particularly known areas of storage such as pockets and waistbands. This does not take long, and it uses the natural sensitivity of the palms, putting you in good position to avoid a "sharps" incident. A preliminary external pat of pockets warns you of possible hazards prior to investigating the contents.

Once this is done, I recommend slowly turning the pockets inside out, bringing the items to you and in full view, rather than opening it wide, shining a flashlight, and hoping to see hazards. Bringing them to you will give you a better view and, again, help to avoid hazardous incidents. There will be no contamination issue with the ground because the item was already there and already has any elements from that immediate area. In doing this, it is quite possible to locate something of immediate value to the investigation that might otherwise not be as timely.

What To Do If You Alter, Move, Or Destroy Evidence

Finally, for anyone involved in any phase of crime scene investigation, the goal of all concerned is to preserve all evidence at the scene. Various concepts and methods have been discussed, such as intentional planning, evidence evaluation strategies, the importance of asking the right question, do's and don'ts, as well as ways to address errors of various degrees when faced with the situation in courtroom testimony. One concept that does not fall neatly into any chapter is the concept of intentional but explainable evidence destruction. Now, this may seem like an oxymoron to some and outright sacrilege to others. However, a truth that is held by many is that it is permissible to alter, move, or destroy evidence as long as the reason for any of those actions is the active pursuit of the primary goals of police work: preservation of life, apprehension of a suspect, and/or recovery of property.

The classic example, noted in an earlier chapter, is that of a police officer rushing the police vehicle directly into a scene to rescue an injured and bleeding victim, running over the suspect's gun and expended shell casings in the process. This can be openly documented and stated quite plainly in any report and courtroom. State openly that evidence was destroyed, along with the reason that it was. The same is true whether evidence was altered or moved. There can be legitimate reasons for doing so, which are directly related to the three main goals. Most readers certainly can think of a situation where such a thing happened at a scene, and there may have been attempts to repair the damage in some way. Replacing evidence never goes well; it is a bad idea because, no matter the apparent intent, it is still staging a scene or, worse, recreating evidence. It is better to lose a case and maintain departmental integrity. In reality, the criminal justice system (and all of its parts) will forgive such events if the primary reason for the action is the preservation of life or the immediate apprehension of the suspect. It is the main reason we do what we do.

Chapter 13

Final Thoughts

Chapter Outline

ABSTRACT

This concluding chapter discusses recommendations presented in the book, provides additional resources for the reader, and includes a final note of encouragement to forensic practitioners.

KEYWORDS: Forensic mindset; Leadership and self-deception.

And yet one more solution to the issues raised

At the beginning of this book, I said that the obvious cannot be overstated. Part of that "obvious" was to note that everyone involved in crime scene investigations has the goal of finding the evidence and processing it correctly. Forensic professionals also have been compelled to "work smarter" because of shrinking resources that affect the time, talent, and resources available for those investigations. It was my intention to provide a framework to indicate when one can be working smarter, as well as examples of what working smarter looks like in an investigation.

I also suggested that we establish a productive epistemology of crime scene processing—that is, an approach in which we are consciously aware of our own thoughts and decision-making processes and, subsequently, their present and future impact on a given scene. This is a problem-solving approach rather than a blame approach. These are the factors that lead to a *forensic mindset*. If you have gotten to this point in the book, then you have allowed me to provide tools to examine your own paradigm of investigative philosophy. For that, I am appreciative.

I also wish to recommend an additional resource book, *Leadership and Self-Deception*, by the Arbinger Institute—the description of which I will paraphrase from the jacket cover. Using a story format, the book illustrates ways in which we blind ourselves, whether at work or at home, and how that process has the impact of inhibiting and even sabotaging our success and best efforts—certainly the very thing we need to avoid in crime scene investigations. These negatives can happen even when we have the best of intentions and can inhibit even the most well-trained and well-intentioned teams, as has been seen, for example, in the case study in Chapter 6. *Leadership and Self-Deception* gives a comprehensive framework for accessing your innate positive abilities, which can greatly improve your crime scene investigations as well as other facets of your personal and professional lives. My endorsement and recommendation of the work *Leadership and Self-Development* is by permission of the Arbinger Institute, the author of the book. Their permission does not constitute an endorsement by the institute of this book.

A NOTE OF ENCOURAGEMENT

The job of police work, in whatever aspect one is serving, is not for the faint of heart, the unwilling, or the uncommitted. The ongoing economic situation has forced most, if not all, forensic units to accomplish their respective missions with fewer resources than before, including personnel. Events such as the Boston Marathon bombing may be giving us an unwelcome view into the future of the types of incidents that we may be compelled to deal with much more often— incidents that may very well be powered or inspired by various conflicts and events around the world. The challenges to police work in general, and the forensic community in particular, are far greater than when I started many years ago. There also are so many things done right in the field of criminal investigations that it would take multiple volumes to note them all. In my view, it is safe to say that you are, most likely, already doing those right things. It is my hope that this work provides a framework that helps this field to meet the ongoing and future challenges we must face, using an analysis of the systemic issues that threaten the very good work we already do and provide a more productive pathway that avoids those issues. Forensics will continue to be a hard job to do, and I am certain that it will only get more difficult as time and events press forward. However, if the job was easy, everyone would be doing it. Instead, it is hard, very hard...and so you are.

The obvious cannot be overstated.

Index

Note: Page number "f" indicate figures.

Printed in the United States
By Bookmasters